THE CENTRA
LUDWIG WIT

D1649906

Gerd Brand

THE CENTRAL TEXTS OF
LUDWIG WITTGENSTEIN

Translated and with an Introduction by
Robert E. Innis

Basil Blackwell · Oxford

First published in the United Kingdom 1979 by
Basil Blackwell Publisher Ltd.
5 Alfred Street, Oxford, England OX1 4HB

Originally published in German under the title
Die Grundlegenden Texte von Ludwig Wittgenstein by
Suhrkamp verlag, Frankfurt am Main 1975.

ISBN 0 631 10921 8 Hardback
     0 631 10931 5 Paperback.

Printed in Great Britain by
Western Printing Services Ltd, Bristol

CONTENTS

TRANSLATOR'S INTRODUCTION

Robert E. Innis

In this book the linguistic turn of Wittgenstein encounters the phenomenological turn of Husserl. Both programmes in twentieth-century philosophy have generated their own internal history and both have suffered internal divisions, revisions, and expansions. A large volume of commentaries has been produced to explicate the internal lines of forces of both traditions, and orthodoxies of interpretation have arisen to safeguard the original deposit, while heretics and eclectics of every sort have appealed to texts and selections of texts to support their positions. This characterization applies as much to the Wittgensteinian as to the Husserlian heritage.[1]

What Brand has tried to do, however, is not to produce another commentary and to enter the lists to challenge all and sundry with his interpretation, but perhaps more radically, to offer a cross-section of topics around which Wittgenstein's thought circled from the very beginning and which informed the total course of his philosophizing. It is an ingenious attempt to construct a systematic framework for a text-immanent reading of the total work of Wittgenstein. Although no texts really 'speak for themselves' the present selection, collation, and paraphrasing of texts from the Wittgensteinian corpus comes fairly close to that impossible hermeneutical ideal. The chief peculiarity of the book is the combination of actual textual citation with a close paraphrase which, while Brand's words, keeps very close to the words of Wittgenstein himself. The fundamental assumption running throughout the collection is that one can truly collate the various themes in Wittgenstein's work, treating them as if they had been subjected to phenomenological analysis by Wittgenstein himself. Readers will have to decide for themselves whether a hermeneutical violence has been done to the inner unity of Wittgenstein's philosophizing or whether a non-existent unity has been imposed on the texts by Brand's procedure.

Because of the text-immanent procedure adopted by Brand I would like, in a brief and schematic way, to point out certain aspects of the present book which gear into issues and contexts which could not be developed in the course of the book itself. My comments are in no way meant to offer a guide to the present book, which is itself meant to be a guide to Wittgenstein, but merely to offer some indications for reflection and further inquiry.

In Wittgenstein's case the turn to language and its thematization had both substantive and methodological grounds. His principal early concern was with what could be said and with the logical structure of discourse. At the same time, as is clear already from the notebooks of 1914–17, Wittgenstein was perplexed especially by the possibility of delineating by a radical reflection upon the webs of discourse the great mysteries of subjectivity, of will, of value, of religion and the mystical, all of which have been phenomenological themes.[2] Thus, the great problematic of the *limit* and the persistent dialectic of *saying and showing*. The unsaid and the unutterable also lay at the foundations of Wittgenstein's work in philosophy.[3]

Even before Wittgenstein a certain kind of philosophy had taken a specifically linguistic turn with the work of Frege, Whitehead and Russell.[4] Language, with its articulate structure, presents the indispensable instrument of thought and by its power of reflexivity it is able to turn back upon itself and subject itself to systematic analysis. In his own way and with his own specific emphases Wittgenstein continued, though with radically different motivation, this kind of analysis. However, a systematic presentation of his later work as well as an explicit and point-by-point confrontation with his putatively repudiated early work forever eluded his grasp.

Wittgenstein's work was constantly characterized by a thoroughgoing anti-psychologism, and, in fact, a repudiation of any primacy or even possibility of reflection upon consciousness or synthesis such as one finds in the tradition of transcendental philosophy. He was adamantly opposed to having recourse to the realm of the mental as a court of last resort, to the beetle in the box. However, Wittgenstein's writings are filled with analyses of issues of great importance to psychology and to that weird discipline of the so-called philosophy of mind, with its recourse to acts, intentions, states, attendings, habits, and so forth. But Wittgenstein undertook to study them by reflecting on language and on the grammar of expressions in which these items are either incorporated or manifested. Thus the significance of Wittgenstein's dictum that 'grammar tells us what kind of thing an object is.'

Paradoxically it is the very insistence on language and the logical grammar of expressions (and the cognate procedure of analysing examples) that has given, in effect, the phenomenological tone to Wittgenstein's work after the earlier and linguistically spare treatments of the *Notebooks* and *Tractatus Logico-Philosophicus*. Explanation must cease and description alone must take its place. The method of models, of the production of perspicuous representations, was meant to light up and make present the essential contours of the heterogeneous forms of life in which human living is embodied. With its concentration on language-games and forms of life the Wittgensteinian operation attained its phenomenological character, but without the systematic egological and transcendental aspects of Husserl's work.

Husserl's project shared with Wittgenstein's a certain topological or topographical character. The intention was to *sort out* the phenomena. The sorting was for Wittgenstein a 'grammatical' one, while for Husserl it became a thorough inventory of the forms of consciousness. Now what both men emphasized, in their own writings at least, was that one of the central keys to the structure of the mind, and of the self, was a reflection upon *expressions*. Expressions became the mediating terms of access not just to the objective realm, to the various domains of cognitive, practical, and affective life, but also to the subjective realm, the domain of the source, of the self as limit, to, in Husserl's term, world constituting subjectivity. The operations of subjectivity were already thematized by Husserl in the *Logical Investigations* along the model of expressions. One went from the expression, which manifested its own objective logical grammar, to the lived *act* which generated it, which was its origin. Thus, in this sense, language – the realm of the said – became the transcendental clue to subjectivity.[5]

However, with Husserl the intention remained of giving a theoretical (albeit descriptive) account of subjectivity as an

autonomous region. Thus, consciousness itself was to be
thematized as it was in itself, but without any concession to
psychologism, whose destruction was one of Husserl's principal
early goals. Husserl was interested in the invariant, structural,
eidetic aspects of consciousness, in, so to speak, its *logical*
structures. But he had no aversion, as Wittgenstein did, to
having recourse to consciousness as such as a thematic concern.
In fact, while Wittgenstein eschewed all direct analyses of consciousness, such as we have in, for example, the *Cartesian
Meditations*, his investigations of intentions, feelings, certainty,
seeing-as, givenness, and so forth, in effect constitute a phenomenology of consciousness, while the discussions of family-
resemblances, of multifarious examples, of forms of life and
language-games, parallel, in their objective and descriptive
thrust, the noematic concerns of Husserl's phenomenology.

Both the noetic, subjectively oriented analyses as well as the
noematic, content-oriented, analyses of Husserl were under a
pressing necessity to be systematic. Husserl could not admit –
as Wittgenstein did – that he was simply concerned with bits
and pieces of 'natural history' dealing with mankind. He was in
search of the *radical grounds* of all human intercourse in the
world. Or, as Husserl put it when asked what the really guiding
question of his life-work was, the problem was 'the origin of the
world'. Phenomenology, as the science of sciences, was to chart
this genesis and to trace it back to the functions of a constituting
subjectivity.[6] Indeed, as a science of sciences, it was meant to
uncover the ultimate conditions and principles, in the sense of
archai, in accordance with which the world, as a matrix of sense
and relevance, arose and *appeared* to consciousness. The
extraordinary scope and difficulty of such an undertaking led
Husserl to develop the complicated methodological apparatus
and procedures for his simultaneously subjective and objective
analyses.

But the systematic exigence in Husserl's work involved also
an impossibility of repudiating philosophy's theoretical intentions. Now a specifically *therapeutic* intention lay at the very
heart of Wittgenstein's project and his goal was not really – at
least thematically – to develop a philosophy of philosophies but
to *dissolve* philosophical problems, and to do so by laying bare
the misleading analogies, the grammatical mistakes, the pieces

of nonsense embedded in our language and against which we are constantly bumping our heads, like a fly flitting around in a fly-bottle.[7] Expressly, then, Wittgenstein wanted to replace theory by therapy and this goal gave, for temperamental reasons too, the broken and fragmented literary form to his work. At the same time, since the problems Wittgenstein was grappling with were so monumental and involuted, Wittgenstein's writings have a fertile heuristic value. They are a veritable quarry not just of enigmatic and dark sayings, but of hints, allusions, pointers, and illuminating models and examples. Hence the search for perspicuous representations and sets of intermediate examples, paralleling Husserlian techniques of imaginal variations.

Brand has managed, it seems to me, to perform the useful hermeneutical task of bridging the gap between the descriptive or phenomenological thrust of Wittgenstein's work and his deepest therapeutic intent, and he has done so by laying bare the multiple foci which give an overarching inner unity to Wittgenstein's life-long reflective practice. The shifts and turns of Wittgenstein's way are recognized but it is shown, quite clearly I think, that there was truly something *about which* Wittgenstein thought. Indeed, if Brand's reading of Wittgenstein is correct, Wittgenstein's self-interpretation of both his procedures and his significance cannot be accepted as final. Rather, Wittgenstein becomes one more important figure in a long tradition of philosophical reflection who deals, albeit in radically altered form, with determinate and common problems. One can also see remarkable parallels not just to the Husserl who governs this 'reading' of Wittgenstein but to others. I would like to mention three in particular as guides to further reading.

A first parallel that could be pursued is with C. S. Peirce. Like Wittgenstein Peirce engaged in a radical critique of immediacy and of the pursuit of certitude. Just as with Peirce consciousness becomes, in its most fundamental aspect, an infinite process of working with signs, consequently a differentiated process of semiosis, such that there is no last link in a chain of interpretations to *ground* or *found* knowing or intercourse with the world, so in Wittgenstein there is no *fundamentum inconcussum* other than the forms of life and language-games in which we find ourselves. We can touch bedrock, to be sure, but our spade is turned when we recognize there is no standpoint which is not truly a stand*point*, one among many. The semiotic transformation of philosophy in Peirce, with the consequence that philosophy becomes a phenomenology of sign- and meaning-systems – correlated with the central idea of habit – has its analogue in Wittgenstein's concern with philosophical grammar and his discovery that the 'world' is a complex matrix of referential totalities (of language-games and their attendant and interwoven forms of life) and that philosophy is just one form of life, and language-game, among others. I think that the reader of the following book could profitably study the parallels between Peirce's and Wittgenstein's critiques of immediacy, between their notions of an object, between the role of rules in both men, their correlative notions of the subject and its mode of givenness, of the impossibility of escaping from interpretation, and so forth.[8]

A second illuminative parallel is with H.-G. Gadamer's project of a philosophical hermeneutics.[9] It has become a commonplace to point out the areas of contact between Wittgenstein and Heidegger, though it is never quite clear whether the 'early' or 'later' Heidegger is the most important and fertile reference. However, the transformation of Heidegger by Gadamer, which in my opinion is of far more interest, relevance, and theoretical value than Heidegger's work itself, ought to be considered alongside the Wittgensteinian project. Gadamer's great problem is the 'linguistic constitution' of the world and the intrinsically language-constituted nature of human understanding of and comportment in the world. Language functions as so many prisms through which the light of the world is mediated to us, and the task of a philosophical hermeneutics is to *retrieve*, by persistent interpretative projections, the past authentic meanings of our tradition and to apply them to the circle of meanings in which we dwell. Gadamer himself has pointed out that when he first began to read Wittgenstein the notion of a language-game, a *Sprachspiel*, came most naturally to him. Indeed, one of the great central organizing categories of Gadamer's work has been that of *Spiel*, though it is not clear whether it should be rendered more appropriately as *play* or *game*. At any rate, the analogy is striking between the interpretative moves of a philosophical hermeneutics which studies the interpretative moves of other hermeneutical projects and Wittgenstein's study of the various 'moves' constituting the grammars of multifarious and heterogeneous language-games.

Gadamer's framework, however, is self-consciously situated within the whole tradition of Western philosophical thinking and he has pursued in elegant and clear form and with methodological awareness the variety of topics to which his attention has been directed. The provenance of Wittgenstein's problems – and even of his methodological procedures – was quite limited, though we now know, through the gigantic work of Garth Hallett, that the base of Wittgenstein's philosophizing was much more differentiated than he intimated or than one can gather, strictly speaking, from references in his own writings. Reading Gadamer along with Wittgenstein and reflecting upon the extensive historical and hermeneutical matrix of his work should enable one to see more clearly the scope and originality of Wittgenstein's own analyses and will perhaps help to forge another link between Wittgenstein and the continental tradition of philosophy. One will see, for instance, the shared concern with the unavoidably interpretative and finite character of our behaviour in the world, the linguistically constituted relativity of our standpoints, and, perhaps most importantly, the dissolution of the pretence of an objective metaphysics functioning as a super-science.

A third parallel that could be pursued is with the work of Michael Polanyi.[10] Polanyi's own references to Wittgenstein are not complimentary, but there are points of substantive overlapping in their own projects. Perhaps the most important is the centrality of the notion of *meaning* and the critique of objectivism (something Polanyi shares with Gadamer, too). Although Polanyi thematically oriented his *later* work around the notion of meaning, already in *Personal Knowledge*[11] he had, on the basis of a systematic generalization of the implications of Gestalt theory, identified meanings with *wholes*, the constitution of which bears remarkable parallels to what Wittgenstein wrote in his discussions of seeing and seeing-as and, in general, of the basic issues in a philosophical treatment of perception.[12] Furthermore, Wittgenstein's discussion of family resemblances parallels Polanyi's discussions of the fusion of incompatibles and the *openness* and flexibility of our conceptual systems (though Polanyi repudiates Waismann's approach with its Kantian overtones). Polanyi's insistence on the *closed* character of our interpretative frameworks, however, recalls Wittgenstein's thesis of the heterogeneous nature of our language-games (there are remarkable parallels in this respect between Gadamer and Polanyi, too).

In fact, the language-problematic lay at the centre of Polanyi's work, and language became the generative source of all specifically human intercourse with the world.[13] Polanyi once wrote: 'All human thought comes into existence by grasping the meaning and mastering the use of language. Little of our mind lives in our natural body; a truly human intellect dwells in us only when our lips shape words and our eyes read print.'[14] Both the giving of sense to and the reading of sense out of our experience is the paradigmatic act of the mind, something we do, a performance, and from early on Polanyi assimilated such performances to the logical structure of a skill, based on the crucial distinction between focal and subsidiary awareness. Polanyi noted that in a skilful performance we integrate a set of particulars upon which we are relying to a focus which we are directly intending. We attend *from* the particulars *to* the focus upon which they bear. This act of integration – paradigmatically exemplified in cases of visual perception – is an 'informal act of the mind' which cannot be replaced by a formal operation. Polanyi once discribed his task as that of tracing language back to its tacit roots. I would like to suggest that a confrontation of Polanyi's thesis of the mental character of meaning with Wittgenstein's putative anti-mentalistic thrust might enrich the Wittgensteinian operation and show from another point of view the reciprocity between 'grammatical' and 'phenomenological' procedures.

The preceding comments are to be taken as heuristic pointers and hints. I have tried in shorthand form to draw attention to certain obvious (to me) parallels that came to mind as I was preparing the English-language version of this book. Other parallels will no doubt come to others' minds as they work through the book. It may be the majority opinion that it is no longer possible to say anything new *about* Wittgenstein. The present book, which is not about Wittgenstein, with its ingenious schematization and interpretative grid, may raise the question, however, whether Wittgenstein himself can be heard to be saying something new.

A note on translations: I have consulted and utilized existing translations in rendering the present book into English, but I have not always followed them exactly. Often the translations have been modified, sometimes extensively, sometimes in minor details and phrasing. My principal goal has been to produce an idiomatic version that respects both the actual Wittgenstein texts cited in the book and Brand's paraphrase, which has numerous overtones not found in the general translations of Wittgenstein's opus. I would like to thank Professor Harald Reiche of MIT for his advice and help concerning certain thorny German passages and my wife, Marianne, for aid in editing the index of citations and references.

NOTES

[1] A masterly and massive discusion of the encounter between the linguistic and phenomenological turns can be found in the extremely important work of Ernst Tugendhat, *Vorlesungen zur Einführung in die sprachanalytische Philosophie* (Frankfurt-am-Main: Suhrkamp Verlag, 1976).

[2] A useful bibliographical guide to these issues in phenomenology can be found in Stewart and Mickunas, *Exploring Phenomenology* (Chicago: American Library Association, 1974).

[3] Although W. W. Bartley III's book is seriously flawed, he does insist on the centrality of these topics in Wittgenstein's work. Cf. also S. Toulmin and A. Janik, *Wittgenstein's Vienna* (New York: Simon and Schuster, 1973).

[4] John Passmore's *A Hundred Years of Philosophy* (Baltimore: Penguin Books, 1968) is a good guide and supplies bibliographical materials.

[5] This is brought out in the most lucid fashion by René Schérer in his *La phénoménologie des 'Recherches logiques' de Husserl* (Paris: Presses Universitaires de France, 1967). The later work, *Formal and Transcendental Logic*, translated by Dorion Cairns (The Hague: Martinus Nijhoff, 1969), also places language at the centre of a phenomenological project. Cf. also André de Muralt's fine work on this book, *The Idea of Phenomenology*, translated by Garry L. Breckon (Evanston: Northwestern University Press, 1974), and

Suzanne Bachelard, *A Study of Husserl's 'Formal and Transcendental Logic'*, translated by Lester E. Embree (Evanston: Northwestern University Press, 1968).

[6] This central notion in Husserl's phenomenology has been charted by Robert Sokolowski in *The Formation of Husserl's Concept of Constitution* (The Hague: Martinus Nijhoff, 1970).

[7] Cf. Richard Rorty, *The Linguistic Turn* (Chicago: University of Chicago Press, 1967), and Garth Hallett, *A Companion to Wittgenstein's 'Philosophical Investigations'* (Ithaca: Cornell University Press, 1977), for discussions of this aspect of Wittgenstein's work.

[8] The clearest and certainly the most provocative discussion of these issues can be found in the writings of K.-O. Apel. Cf. his collection *Transformation der Philosophie*, 2 vols (Frankfurt-am-Main: Suhrkamp Verlag, 1973), and his brilliant book on Peirce, *Der Denkweg von C.S. Peirce* (Frankfurt-am-Main: Suhrkamp, 1975).

[9] Gadamer's masterwork, *Truth and Method*, is now available in in an English-language version, even if somewhat inadequately (New York: Seabury Press, 1975), and a selection of his papers, *Philosophical Hermeneutics*, ed. David Linge (Berkeley: University of California Press, 1976), can also be usefully consulted. Cf. my review-article on *Truth and Method* in *The Thomist*, XL, 2 (1976), pp. 311–21.

[10] Some of these points of overlapping are discussed by Cahal Daly, 'Polanyi and Wittgenstein', in *Intellect and Hope*, ed. Thomas A. Langford and William H. Poteat (Durham: Duke University Press, 1968).

[11] Chicago: University of Chicago Press, 1958.

[12] The perceptual model is subjected to analysis and evaluation in my 'Polanyi's Model of Mental Acts', in *The New Scholasticism*, XLVII, 2 (1973), pp. 147–78 and in 'Tacit Knowing and Gestalt Theory', an unpublished manuscript.

[13] Cf. my 'Meaning, Thought and Language in Polanyi's Epistemology', *Philosophy Today*, 18 (1974), pp. 47–67, as well as my lecture 'Polanyi's Epistemology and the Philosophy of Language' given at Skidmore College at the Conference on the Relevance of Polanyi's Thought to the Various Disciplines.

[14] 'Tacit Knowing: Its Bearing on Some Problems of Philosophy', *Knowing and Being*, ed. Marjorie Grene (Chicago: University of Chicago Press, 1969), p. 160.

ABBREVIATIONS

BGB   'Bemerkungen über Frazers "The Golden Bough"', in *Synthese* 17, 1967, pp. 233–53.

BB   *The Blue and Brown Books*, Basil Blackwell, 1958.

E   'A Lecture on Ethics', in *The Philosophical Review* 74, 1965, pp. 3–12.

LAC   *Lectures and Conversations*, edited by Cyril Barrett, University of California Press, 1967.

NB   *Notebooks 1914–16*, Basil Blackwell, 1961.

NFL   'Wittgenstein's Notes for Lectures on "Private Experience" and "Sense Data",' edited by Rush Rhees, in *The Philosophical Review* 77, 1968, pp. 271–320.

OC   *On Certainty*, Basil Blackwell, 1969.

PG   *Philosophical Grammar*, Basil Blackwell, 1974.

PI   *Philosophical Investigations*, Basil Blackwell, 1953.

PR   *Philosophical Remarks*, Basil Blackwell, 1975.

RFM *Remarks on the Foundations of Mathematics*, Basil Blackwell, 1956.

T   *Tractatus Logico-Philosophicus*, Routledge and Kegan Paul, 1961.

W   Waismann, Friedrich, *Wittgenstein und der Wiener Kreis*, shorthand notes of F. Waismann, ed. McGuinness, Basil Blackwell, 1967.

Z   *Zettel*, Basil Blackwell, 1969.

Since Wittgenstein wrote for the most part in numbered paragraphs, the references in the text refer to them except where a page number is expressly noted, such as in the cases of *The Blue and Brown Books*, the second half of the *Philosophical Investigations*, and so forth.

B

FOREWORD

'After several unsuccessful attempts to weld my results together into such a whole, I realized that I should never succeed. The best that I could write would never be more than philosophical remarks; my thoughts were soon crippled if I tried to force them on in any single direction against their natural inclination' (PI ix).

We can see from this assertion of Ludwig Wittgenstein that he was clear about the two fundamental characteristics which marked the manner of presentation – note: the manner of presentation – of his thought. His presentations are, except in *Tractatus Logico-Philosophicus*, fragmentary, concentrated on single problems, and unsystematic. Even where he expended the greatest effort to bring his comments into a definite sequence for publication, except for smaller groupings no systematic unity is recognizable. Indeed, even in individual comments which are characterized as individual because he numbers them, Wittgenstein sometimes lets himself be distracted from the initial question in order to treat other problems which emerge in the course of his reflection. Even in the individual comment, therefore, the presentation is not always closed off.

If, besides, one adverts to and considers the fact that in his late work Wittgenstein explicitly questioned or rejected many of his earlier thoughts, it cannot be a matter of amazement that it is difficult to understand his thought if one wants to see it in its larger contexts. On the other hand, his comments, taken singly and also in groups, often evoke spirited agreement on account of their freshness, their disconcerting formulations, their sharpness and clarity, their critical power and their insight.

This explains to a certain degree the fascination and the influence which Wittgenstein exercises, as well as the often somewhat remarkably suppositional character of Wittgensteinian interpretation. Many Wittgenstein interpreters say about his philosophy, by which they are always fascinated, that it is in some parts dark, enigmatical, and incomprehensible.

That is the case even for the *Tractatus*. The interpreters we are referring to here, but not only they, are of the opinion that Wittgenstein so neglected the general for the sake of the particular that his philosophy, as an accumulation of sparkling, detailed language descriptions, as an involvement with the nuances of the specific, resembles more an art than a science. Russell even goes so far as to say that Wittgenstein's efforts after the *Tractatus* are trivial or ungrounded and had nothing to do with philosophy, and that their concern is an unimportant investigation of language which has no connection whatsoever with the investigation of logic, of knowledge, and of reality, which Russell held to be the genuine task of philosophy (B. Russell, *My Philosophical Development*, London 1959, pp. 216f). Finally, there are many Wittgenstein interpreters who highlight the developments of individual problems in the framework of his total work; often, while they compare his early with his late philosophy, sometimes in the process several 'intermediate' phases also intervene. What we get, in the last analysis, are erratic blocks of material, Wittgenstein orphans, as it were, lying around on the field of interpretation.

Is one not forced, then, to make an attempt at a hitherto unaccustomed interpretation? An interpretation which does not concern itself respectively with different works, or problems which singly thread themselves throughout these works, but one which tries to present Wittgenstein's thought all together and in its inner unity? An interpretation which then perhaps would reveal many apparently obscure points?

Certainly Wittgenstein himself did not present his philosophy as a system. Still the question is forced upon us whether a philosopher, who over a period of decades meditated on and wrote about an always cohesive set of topics, does not have a fundamental and unified system, even if he does not himself describe or articulate it. Especially if he explicitly establishes in his last work that there is no belief, no knowing, no argument outside of a system and that a system is the life-element of arguments (see OC 141, 142, 410, 102, 105). At least one will have to admit that Wittgenstein's philosophizing has an 'approach' that remains unified throughout his transformations. If we want to be careful, therefore, then we can at least ask: how, then, does the style of his procedure and, therefore, the inner unity of his philosophizing come to appearance? Only one person can give the answer to this question, and that is Wittgenstein himself.

In order to get the answer we have to make the attempt to assemble related and correlated themes, thereby considering Wittgenstein's total work, and we must cite or paraphrase the corresponding passages. I use the word 'paraphrase' here because I want to keep quite close to Wittgenstein's text (therefore I use as a reference device not the usual cf. but rather the word 'see'). Even where the paraphrase could be considered by closer explication to be an interpretation, then this so-called interpretation wants to remain Wittgenstein-immanent, not to go beyond his text or to drag in anything from the outside.

My text is to be read, together with the Wittgenstein citations, as one text. In the reading one can, to be sure, leave to the side the quotation marks enclosing the Wittgenstein citations. For this reason I have also retained within my text the I-form; for that is Wittgenstein's way of speaking and this, too, should be presented.

In order to make my intention clear I would like to illustrate it with the following reference. Edmund Husserl often handed over to his assistants a bundle of more or less inter-related manuscripts along with the charge of preparing them for publication under his name. The best-known example is the work *Experience and Judgement*, published under Husserl's name by Ludwig Landgrebe. The comparison breaks down only because due to Wittgenstein's temperament such a thing would have been impossible.

Wittgenstein's thought is at times concentrated on single problems even where he puts his remarks together in larger contexts. That is, the remarks are lined up one after the other, and that they belong together becomes more or less sharply evident; likewise the seriation is discontinuous, and there are often no connections between the single remarks. With every effort to elaborate the continuity and the inner connections of Wittgenstein's thought it is not possible to completely overcome this discontinuity if we want to remain Wittgenstein-immanent. Wittgenstein's style, which should be retained, does not allow this.

As Wittgenstein put it, a system is something in which all the parts point towards one another, in which conclusions and premisses mutually support one another (see OC 142). But a system cannot be presented all at once. Therefore, the method of presentation already demands a successive development in which it is completely natural that one should first of all evince the object of one's belief, so that it will make more intelligible what one is accordingly doing. The problems which accompany such a procedure are well known to all those who have to work in philosophy. The systematization of the presentation will never correspond completely to the system being presented. But it can furnish more or less good entrances into the system. The attempt here is to lay open the approaches to Wittgenstein's system as well as possible, and to then give it a presentation.

Such a procedure will evoke some protest from followers of Wittgenstein. From some the objection will come that that is un-Wittgensteinian, since Wittgenstein was a foe of every kind of systematization or generalization. The answer to this is that Wittgenstein himself did not at all repudiate a systematization of his philosophy: as the citation at the beginning shows, he did indeed try to give it such a form. That he in the end did not do so is, however, apparently less a question of a thought-system than of temperament.

Wittgenstein also did not repudiate the universal. To assert this would mean to accept the position, already mentioned above, that Wittgenstein's philosophy resembles more an art than a science. This position is weak not only for the reason that its representatives have to admit that – in Wittgenstein's later work too – there is at least implicit generalization, but also because one already needs general grounds in order to put the specific into the foreground; and Wittgenstein gives us these general grounds. His method of adducing many examples also makes this clear; for he openly chooses the examples in regard to a universal notion, for which they are precisely examples. Without the universal or general element it would be senseless to discourse about examples. That means, therefore, only that there are no universals without the particulars, and vice versa. In a foreword I do not want to enter into the question of what exactly is to be understood by the term 'universal'.

The objection will also be raised that positions from different periods of thought are put together here. But in these positions the thought revolves around the same set of themes. Do they not then belong together? And if with a fresh eye one reads them placed together in this way then one sees that they do belong together. If, of course, a later conception uneqivocally rejects an earlier one, then the earlier one is discarded.

There is a difficulty in the fact that the dominant tone of Wittgenstein's late philosophy is essentially critical, not genuinely constructive. In addition, his criticisms are more comprehensive, coherent and systematic than his constructive utterances, which, moreover, are strewn throughout his whole work. The motivation for this is to be found in Wittgenstein's fundamental phenomenological attitude. For him our comprehension is already given, but for the most part distorted. The concern, therefore, is in general not to produce it for the first time but to lay it out in the open (see PG 72). The way of a 'destructive exposition' as the method of presentation is, therefore, outlined in advance by our fundamental situation. And precisely because our authentic comprehension is often skewed we have to first of all clear away the dissimulation before we can at all see the truth. We also come more easily to the point of better understanding what we are really dealing with here if we arrive at a genuine understanding by going through the dissimulations and distortions instead of simply giving a presentation of this understanding itself. We often also overlook the truth which lies in front of us, or it appears to us as trivial. It is only in contrast to the error that has been overcome that we see the truth in its whole light. Finally, we scarcely go from truth to error. Since error, however, is what we are mainly dealing with, we have to set out from error in order to arrive at truth. For otherwise beside the discovered truth the errors could persist. 'One has to start from error and show it the truth. That is, one has to uncover the source of error, otherwise hearing the truth is of no use to us. Truth cannot enter by force if something else takes its place.

'To convince someone of the truth it is not adequate to establish the truth. One has to find the *way* from error to truth' (BGB, p. 234).

It is likewise important to develop authentic understanding itself. Such is the special task of this work: to put into the foreground the constructive aspects of Wittgenstein's philosophy, and also especially their inner connection with the critical aspects.

Sometimes in the presentation contradictions emerge, questions and hesitations, sliding from one sense to another. In this way problems come to light. Because the present work is intended to adhere strictly to the Wittgensteinian text these problems are not solved. What nevertheless is attempted is to bring the texts into an inner unity which will let the emerging problems become evident, and do so in a systematic framework. The solution of these problems themselves is a task of genuine Wittgenstein interpretation and of philosophical criticism. It can be no task of a Wittgenstein presentation, and that alone is the concern of the present text. That the text, however, for all its abridgement, is in fact a Wittgenstein presentation, has to be shown by the book itself.

In the attempt to present Wittgenstein's system gaps become evident. The procedure of putting elements together has such a consequence pre-eminently, in that in one part open questions become especially conspicuous, while they can be directly answered only in another part. Since one is dealing, therefore, with gaps within a system – there are gaps only within a system (see PR 157, 158) – it is understandable that one make some attempts to close these gaps. Worthwhile stimuli for further work in a Wittgensteinian style have their origin here.

Many of Wittgenstein's remarks are just as illuminating as they are also enigmatic and of a veiled clarity. If, in the present situation, we were to try to clarify their puzzling character, through interpretation and continuation, then, first of all, we would no more remain Wittgenstein-immanent, but, secondly, the revealing power of the original Wittgensteinian expressions would also be interpreted away.

The kind of procedure I have chosen has the disadvantage that it does not close the gaps or build bridges by interpretations, explications and references. This disadvantage is balanced by the advantage of keeping strictly to Wittgenstein. In this way the text can now and then remain open for interpretations; under certain circumstances several interpretations are possible; it may be too that new interpretations, other than those customary up to now, will be demanded. But on the whole the philosophy of Wittgenstein can be better understood by means of the presentation I have chosen. It becomes clearer in its articulation and more stringent in its comprehensive argumentation. Also, what as a separate remark would appear as obscure and less intelligible often becomes clearer and more intelligible.

Certainly some Wittgenstein experts will say: I would have put the texts together in quite another way, or: I would have made a different choice, or both. But the reason for that lies solely in the fact that Wittgenstein thought very much in circles. What is essential however is that one attempt be made at any rate to construct such an assembly of texts which encompass the totality of his work. In this way this book will offer to those interested in Wittgenstein, in any case, new material and new provocations, and will show ways one can further philosophize with Wittgenstein beyond Wittgenstein. 'I should not like my writing to spare other people the trouble of thinking. But, if possible, to stimulate someone to thoughts of his own' (Foreword to PI).

Finally one will rightly ask what then my own view of Wittgenstein is, since my presentation certainly depends on it. I see in Wittgenstein an excellent representative of a phenomenology of the life-world. Wittgenstein's thought moves between two poles: 'such and such is the case' and 'such and such is being done'. How things are and what is being done are *shown*, are grasped *in the activity* itself, are, in the last analysis, given to us in perceptible *forms of life*. That on this foundation – even if only in fragments which are important and elemental – there is possible a revealing description of how men understand the world and how they operate in it – therefore a phenomenology of the life-world – appears to me to be plausibility itself. Wittgenstein stands on the ground of a revelatory all-grounding (including itself) naiveté (therefore we use quite calmly the word 'transcendental'), proceeding by means of a destructive and exhibiting analysis. So, for me, Wittgenstein is a phenomenologist purely and simply.

A

CERTAINTY

I

1 An important concern of philosophy is to furnish a reliable foundation for our understanding. In the foundations of our knowledge, however, we discover gaps and brittleness. The gaps and the brittleness are manifest in doubt. One would like, therefore, to take the path of doubting everything so as to attain to a more secure foundation of understanding which can be got from the elimination of doubt. 'It may easily look as if every doubt merely *revealed* an existing gap in the foundations; so that secure understanding is only possible if we first doubt everything that *can* be doubted, and then remove all these doubts' (PI 87). Nevertheless, one immediately discovers that it is not possible to doubt everything and then eliminate the doubt, but rather that doubt itself, as such, presupposes something that cannot be doubted. One discovers that I do not first have to find something indubitable, but that it is already there, before doubt. Doubt and its elimination do not first bring forth a genuinely secure understanding, but point to the fact that such is already always there.

2 That something is not in doubt is manifest in action. Let us take as an example an action in which something could be doubted and which is very familiar to us: an order, for example: 'bring me a book.' I can be in doubt whether what I am bringing is really a book. But I can check it by, for example, looking up what the word 'book' means. If I do not know precisely what a book is, then, however, I do know what this or that word means which I find by looking it up, and I know how it is used. The removal of doubt is, therefore, a fact of experience.

And just in this way is it a fact of experience that something is first of all given, even if I doubt it; that, therefore, this object is a book, even if I doubt it.

In order, therefore, to be able to obey a rule I have to be certain about a fact of experience.

3   To obey an order is a meaningful action. The example shows that perhaps in no single instance can I state what has to be beyond doubt, but rather that as a rule judgements of experience have to be beyond doubt if there is to be meaningful action. That means that we already start out from the experimental fact that judgements of experience are beyond doubt (see OC 519). Perhaps the object which I intend does not exist at all. But if one object does not exist, then one still uses somewhere one which does (see OC 56). The example also shows that if I put anything at all to the test I presuppose something which is not tested (see OC 162).

4   This not-tested is not an un-tested, but something that is simply beyond doubt. It is like the door hinges which have to stand fast if a door is to turn (see OC 343). Our questions and our doubts themselves rest on the fact that certain propositions are exempt from doubt, 'are, as it were, like hinges on which those turn' (see OC 341).

Besides, that which stands fast for me I have not explicitly learned, but I find *subsequently*, like the axis around which a body rotates. No one has, for example, taught me that my two hands do not disappear if I do not keep them in sight. Not only have I not explicitly learned this proposition, but I also only express it now in order to give sense to my assertions concerning what is beyond doubt (see OC 152, 153).

5   Doubt only exists as doubting conduct. I cannot live with doubting conduct alone. On the contrary, my normal life is for the most part a non-doubting conduct. I do not doubt and also do not consider that I could doubt if I say to my friend, for example: 'close the door', 'take that chair over there' (see OC 7). If I have a doubt, I can put an end to it by making an assumption or coming to a decision (see OC 146). But that I can act in this way presupposes that doubting behaviour exists only by

reason of a non-doubting behaviour, that at the beginning stands not-doubting. I cannot remain with asking why, in an eternal suspension. Judging and acting begin with not-doubting. Only on the basis of trust can I doubt. 'Is there a why? Must I not begin to trust somewhere? That is to say: somewhere I must begin with not-doubting; and that is not, so to speak, hasty but excusable: it is part of judging' (oc 150). And part of action.

6   Because doubt rests on what cannot be doubted, it leads to its own demise. One can say that I cannot arrive at a genuine doubt as long as I want to doubt everything, precisely because doubt presupposes certainty (see oc 115). If I begin with a doubt it itself leads to its demise. If I want to doubt everything I will not at all come to the beginning of doubt.

Our learning has the form: 'That is a violet.' 'That is a table.' If we always had only doubts and were to hear: 'That is perhaps a . . .' then the practical consequence would be that we would learn nothing and then there would also be nothing which we could doubt. One can generally only doubt if one has already learned something that is a certain. 'One can only make an error in calculation if one has learned to calculate' (z 410; see oc 310). So we see: 'A doubt that doubted everything would not be a doubt' (oc 450). He who in general was not certain about anything would also not even be certain of the sense of his words. That is, he could not even express his doubt (see z 114). In order to be a doubt at all, doubt may not be a universal doubt.

7   Certainly doubt exists. Even if there is no universal doubt there is nevertheless doubt in individual cases. That doubt presupposes something indubitable does not just mean that there is no doubt. If I am in doubt I can, on the one hand, take precautionary measures (see oc 621), and, on the other hand, I can proceed to a justification (see oc 192). But both precautionary measures and justifications only have a meaning if they finally come to an end.

A doubt without end is not even a doubt (see oc 625), just as to want to doubt everything means not even coming to doubt.

II

8   Doubting has its own internal limitation. Doubt does not precede everything. If it comes, it comes afterwards. But it also does so only in a restricted way.

There exist logically impossible as well as unreasonable doubts. In the single case that is a difficult thing to distinguish. But let us take a look at what is unreasonable and what is senseless. In order to get clear about this we want to consider how senseless it is to introduce certain doubts into an action. If, for example, something should happen that is apt to awaken doubt, then certainly there would be grounds to put this doubt itself again into doubt. Therefore, I can just stick with my first belief (see OC 516). Or if we assume that a shopkeeper wants to inspect each one of his apples, then does he not have to inspect the first inspection? Such a doubt (about each apple) would, therefore, be senseless (see OC 459).

'There are cases where doubt is unreasonable, but others where it seems logically impossible. And there seems to be no clear boundary between them' (OC 454; see Z 393).

If water were to freeze on the fire I would be totally amazed. Nevertheless I would assume an unknown influence and hand over the inquiry to physics. But other sorts of doubt would drag everything along with them and hurl them into chaos. They intrude upon what is solid in our personal or in our common life. For example, nothing can make me doubt that this person is N.N. whom I have known for years (see OC 613). Or: 'If I were to say: "I have never been on the moon – but I may be mistaken," that would be idiotic' (OC 662). If I were to imagine that things in my surroundings – men and animals – were suddenly to behave in such a manner as they have never before behaved, then I would believe that I have gone crazy (see Z 393).

If, for example, I were to believe that a table stands before me and there is none there, then that would be an error. But I cannot err, and accordingly I cannot doubt, that I have seen and used for many months a certain table. I cannot also be in error if I know that a few days ago I flew to America. Or that I have taken a daily bath in the last months (see OC 674, 675, 415, 417). Even if I am in error about a specific instance, even if I am in doubt in respect to certain details, I nevertheless have the right to say that in this case I cannot be in error (see OC 633).

'I believe that I have forebears, and that every human being has them. I believe that there are various cities, and, quite generally, I believe in the main facts of geography and history. I believe that the earth is a body on whose surface we move and that it no more suddenly disappears or the like than any other solid body: this table, this house, this tree, etc. If I wanted to doubt the existence of the earth long before my birth, I should have to doubt all sorts of things that I consider established.

'And that I consider something established is not grounded in my stupidity or credulity' (OC 234, 235). The solid (*feststehende*) background of my personal life is the solid ground of common life.

What constitutes the background of our common life is established for everyone. In this steadfast element I come to agreement with others. Indeed, does this common establishment not genuinely show what to be in agreement means? Agreement means not only that what I say agrees with what I am talking about, but that I am in agreement with others about such determinations. I can only err because I am in common agreement with others. For the most part my error first becomes evident on the basis of this conformity. 'In order to make a mistake a man must already judge in conformity with humanity' (OC 156).

What stands fast, that in which we agree, is something that befalls us. For the most part we do not learn it explicitly. I believe that there is a country in which I live, of such and such a shape, that I had great-grandparents, that my parents were in truth my parents, and so on. This steadfast element may never be explicitly uttered as a belief, or thought as a thought, that such is the case. But I can find it if I look for what is steadfast (see OC 334).

And what if I should nevertheless have to change my mind about fundamentals? That is not necessary. Precisely therein consists what is fundamental about these things. 'What if something *really unheard-of* happened? – If, say, I saw houses gradually turning into steam without any obvious cause, if the cattle in the fields stood on their heads and laughed and spoke comprehensible words; if the trees gradually changed into men

and men into trees. Now, was I right when, before all these
things happened, I said: "I know that that's a house" etc., or
simply: "that's a house" etc?' (OC 513). Yes, I was right.
Something fundamental excludes its foundations' as a whole
suddenly experiencing an unheard-of alteration. Even if one
day the most unheard-of things shall happen I would be right to
hang unerringly onto what is fundamental, on the foundation of
which the unheard-of is precisely not that. But I do not imagine
the unheard-of, or at any rate I do not act as if it could happen.
I do not have any practically effective doubts about it.

What now if someone still has doubts about reasonable
things? We can let him doubt in peace, for his doubt will not
show itself in practice (see OC 120).

III

9   The overcoming of doubt lies in the lack of doubt itself that
is given in our action. I have two hands, and I have no doubt
about it. That I use the word 'hand' without scruple shows that
lack of doubt belongs to what is essential in an action. If I here
wanted to begin to doubt I would be standing before the abyss.
The question: 'How do I know . . .' makes the action hesitate
or annuls it (see OC 370). If I were to want to go through a
checklist again and again before every single action in order to
test whether what is necessary for the action is also given, I
would not come around to acting at all. Certainty is not
necessary for acting in the sense that it is established beforehand, but it is given in acting itself. It is immanent in the action.
We can, therefore, confidently say: in the beginning was the
deed (see OC 402). 'Why do I not satisfy myself that I have two
feet when I want to get up from a chair? There is no why.
I simply don't. This is how I act' (OC 148).

10   We say that the grounding and the justification of evidence
comes to an end. 'But the end is not certain propositions'
striking us immediately as true, i.e., it is not a kind of *seeing* on
our part; it is our *acting*, which lies at the bottom of the
language-game' (OC 204).

And here it is peculiar that I can indeed give no reasons for my manner of acting, for example, that I use the word 'hand' in *this* way. In no case could I give a reason which would be as certain as precisely the one which it is meant to ground (see OC 307).

11 I could question time and again, but while I am living I do not question. Living consists precisely in that (see OC 344). The difficult thing consists in letting oneself be satisfied with seeing the groundlessness of our belief (see OC 166).

12 From the ungrounded grounding there follows the determination: 'If the true is the grounded, then the ground is not *true*, nor false' (OC 205).

IV

13 We have to distinguish between the actual lack of doubt and my knowledge of it. Lack of doubt is *given* to me in acting. I am directly cognizant of it in knowing and believing. ' "I know" is supposed to express a relation, not between me and the sense of a proposition (like "I believe") but between me and a fact' (OC 90). So I can replace 'I know' by 'it is known to me as certain that . . .' (see OC 272). Normally we simply say: that is so! Only doubting and reflecting about it lets us elaborate the relation of knowing. 'I am sitting with a philosopher in the garden; he says again and again: "I know that that's a tree" pointing to a tree that is near us. Someone else arrives and hears this, and I tell him: "This man is not insane: we are only philosophizing" ' (OC 467).

Since knowing describes a relation, there is a justification for it (see OC 175). Since knowing expresses a relation, this relation – that is, what is known and that I know it – has to be justified. If I know it, whence do I know it: how do I know it? (See OC 550, 441, 555, 556.) Knowing is not of course supposed to express subjective certainty (see OC 415). If I know something, then I know it and do not only believe it (see OC 406, 407, 408).

14 We distinguish from knowing an immediate, inner state which has not been, or is to be, made to stand explicitly in a

a

relation, the state of belief for which there is no justification
(see OC 175). This is so even if the belief, if it is expressed, is
expressed in the that-form. We are not dealing here with a
knowing-relation in connection with which I make explicit
whence it comes and how it is grounded.

15   Here we clearly run up against a last thing, an incontro-
vertible belief, a total conviction. What does that mean other
than that I am not prepared to let anything whatsoever count
here as a counter-proof, that I have reached a position which
I can hold on to? (See OC 116, 86.)

16   Is it not shown here that in knowing and believing there is
found present an affinity with a decision? (See OC 362.) I only
bring a doubt to an end, that is, through a decisive action. But
on the other hand I cannot at all imagine a doubt attached to
my belief. For then the question is raised: what would I believe
if I did not believe such and such? And for that I have no
system at all (see OC 247).

17   Since belief is an immediate inner state it affects all certain-
ties about myself. 'I can know what another person thinks, but
not what I think.
     'It is correct to say: "I know what you think', and false to
say: "I know what I think"' (see PI, p. 222).

B

WORLD

I

18   We saw first of all that at least one fact must be considered as indubitable for there to be a meaningful action. For we saw that many things are certain for us. If we believe something at all it is not a single fact or a single proposition, but a whole system of propositions (see oc 141, 142).

If, for example, we engage in argument, then that occurs only in the framework of a system. At the same time the system is implicit in every argument. 'All testing, all confirmation and disconfirmation of a hypothesis takes place already within a system. And this system is not a more or less arbitrary and doubtful point of departure for all our arguments: no, it belongs to the essence of what we call an argument. The system is not so much the point of departure, as the element in which arguments have their life' (oc 105).

So everything that is and thereby everything which I could doubt stands against the background of a total relational system and is enclosed in it. Our knowing and our convictions, our belief, form a system, a structure (see oc 410; oc 102). And it is only in this system that the individual has the value that we put on it and that it has latent relations which belong to it without being explicit. So, for example, I know that no flight of steps leads from this house six stories deep into the ground, although I have never thought about it (see oc 398). I can discover it, because it lies in my system.

19   Where do I get this total system which I call my world picture? Because I have convinced myself of its correctness, or perhaps also only because I am convinced by its correctness?

No, the background against which I can distinguish in general between true and false is the background which befalls us (see OC 94).

The handed-down background of true and false as indubitable total system, as what stands fast, we call the world.

The handed-down world is a world which I have in common with others. I do not doubt for the simple reason that I am in agreement with others (see OC 280, 281). Not only do I believe in the world that has been handed down, but the others do too. 'Or perhaps I *believe* that they believe it' (OC 288; see OC 289).

20 The world is unquestioned and indubitable. I can no longer doubt it, I can no longer put it into question, for it is precisely what first makes possible every questioning. One can only inquire *from* a standpoint out of which questioning and doubt are possible (see PR 168). But one can no longer inquire after what grounds this standpoint. 'One cannot ask about that initial element which first makes possible every question at all' (PR 168). One cannot ask about the ground of grounds.

21 As unquestioned and indubitable system-ground or as ground-system the world is self-evident to us. This self-evidence makes itself known precisely in the fact that it does not make itself known, that the world is unnoticed. Everything about which we can say something is found in the world, belongs to the world. Language cannot mean anything at all other than the world. Since language cannot mean anything else, the world is not what it first speaks about. The world is self-evident to us. It does not come to our attention, if we look about, move around in space, feel our own bodies, and so on, because there is no radical contrast to the form of our world. The self-evident character of the world is expressed just in the fact that language means only it and can mean only it (see PR 47).

22 I notice something by setting it in opposition to something else. But I cannot set anything in opposition to the world. It contains everything which can be one way or the other.

So the world is also not empirical, but necessary, if by 'empirical' we mean that we can imagine it also as being otherwise. The very existence of the world is, therefore, not empirical. That is, we cannot imagine this existence as being otherwise, and we can also not imagine that the world is not. But an individual thing within the total system of the world we can imagine as other than it is.

II

23 Since the world is unquestioned and necessary, I cannot inquire after it. It is what is given from the beginning which gives to every single thing its sense. That means, every representation really has to do with the world. 'If I say that representation has to do with my world, one cannot say: "because I otherwise would not be able to verify it", but rather because it would otherwise from the very beginning not have any sense for me' (PR 34). In this way, by means of each individual thing, one also understands the world upon which it is founded.

This is clearly shown in examining the problem of how something can be proved. It is evidently not sufficient to say, p can be proved, but one must say: provable according to a definite system. Namely, the proposition p is not provable according to the system S, but it is provable according to *its* system, the system of p. In proving p I understand the system that supports it. 'That p belongs to the system S – that cannot be asserted, but must show itself. One cannot say that p belongs to the system S; one cannot ask to what system p belongs; one cannot look for the system of p; to understand p means to understand its system' (PR 153).

24 Since they are unquestioned, necessary, and pregiven, I cannot draw the limits of my world, but rather limits within my world. We have just shown that we cannot ask whether the proposition p belongs to system S, but rather we can ask whether it belongs to part s of S (see PR 152). But I can consider the world as a fundamental system, and within this fundamental system I can find particular systems, that is, special worlds. 'A system is, so to speak, a world' (PR 152).

The world is already given and the system is already given (and pre-given). Accordingly I cannot look for a system. It can, however, be that a system is given to me implicitly, in certain unwritten symbols. Then I can look for the expression for this system (see PR 152).

25 Here is the place to remark, quite generally, that I never speak *about* systems, but always only *in* systems. If, that is to say, I speak *about* a system, then I am already *in* another system. 'They are precisely what one cannot talk about. Therefore, also what one cannot look for' (PR 152).

Assuming that I had two systems, then I cannot ask about a system which encompasses them both. I cannot, that is to say, *now* look for it. But also if ever one should *show* itself, then I would see that I would never have been able to look for it. It can only show itself (see PR 152). Accordingly, it is also true that something that was unforeseen is not like a gap in a system. It was not foreseeable because the system was simply not yet there. What can be foreseen, and also gaps, only exist in a system. 'What was not seen beforehand was not foreseeable; for one was not in possession of the system in which it could be foreseen. (And would have been foreseen)' (PR 157).

I cannot, therefore, look for the world, because it is a system, and I cannot look for a system, because it, so to speak, is a world.

III

26 Here we have to make a distinction between an experiential whole and a system. The books and chairs in this room, for example, are empirical experiential wholes. Their extension depends upon experience. A system, on the contrary, depends upon the principle upon which it is based (see w, p. 216). Even if I already had all the results for the solution of a problem but find a new way to the solution, then this new way constitutes a new system (see PR 155).

If I construct a fundamental systematic structure, an essential overview, I transgress the empirical domain. I undertake a concept-formation which fashions a stable system.

If I say, for example: 'it will be so' then I leave it it to empirical experience to show me whether it is so. Experience is, however, always already given to me in conceptually structured systems. If I now say: 'it has to be so' then I look upon the context differently; then I form a new concept. The open character of experience, its many possibilities, are closed for the sake of a single possible systematic context, a single possibility (see RFM III-48).

'The limits of the empirical domain – the *formation of concepts*. What transition do I make from "it will be so" to "it *has to* be so"? I form another concept. (. . .)

' "It has to be so" does not mean: "it will be so." On the contrary: "it will be so" chooses one possibility out of others. "It has to be so" considers only *one* possibility' (RFM III-29, 31).

27 While I cannot draw the limits of my world, but can only contemplate systems and objects within them, still these systems or objects can shove themselves into my world, take up its space as it were. A stove can come to be my world. 'As a thing among things, everything is equally insignificant, as a world each one equally significant. If I have been contemplating the stove, and then am told: but now all you know is the stove, my result does indeed seem trivial. For this represents the matter as if I had studied the stove as one among the many things in the world. But if I was contemplating the stove, *it* was my world, and everything else, on the contrary, was pale besides it' (NB, p. 83).

28 I can place over the world a unified descriptive net through which I bring everything to a unitary form. According to the kind of net that I choose there results a kind of world description. If I take various nets then I produce various world descriptions. One such kind of world description is, for example, mechanics.

'Newtonian mechanics, for example, imposes a unified form on the description of the world. Let us imagine a white surface with irregular black spots on it. We then say that whatever kind of pictures these make, I can always approximate as closely as I wish to the description of it by covering the surface with a sufficiently fine square mesh and then saying of every square whether it is black or white. In this way I shall have imposed a unified form on the description of the surface. The form is optional, since I could have achieved the same result by using a net with a triangular or hexagonal mesh. Possibly the use of triangular mesh would have made the description simpler: that is to say, it might be that we could describe the surface more accurately with a coarse triangular mesh than with a fine square mesh (or conversely), and so on. The different nets correspond to different systems for describing the world. Mechanics determines one form or description of the world by saying that all propositions used in the description of the world must be obtained in a given way from a given set of propositions – the axioms of mechanics. It thus supplies the bricks for building the edifice of science, and it says: 'Any building that you want to erect, whatever it may be, must somehow be constructed with these bricks, and with these alone."

'(Just as with the number-system we must be able to write down any number we wish, so with the system of mechanics we must be able to write down any propositions of physics that we wish.)' (T 6.341.)

Here, however, we have to see very clearly that everything that we describe in this way and all laws which we discover treat of the net and not of that which the net describes (see T 6.35).

C

SUBJECT

I

29 The subject is to be distinguished from the world. The question is, how does it appear?

30 If we take the world, first of all, as a visual space, that is, as that towards which we cast our gaze, then we have to establish that the world is first of all given to us without a subject, that is to say, visual space essentially has no owner and contains no indication of a subject (see PR 71). If we see the visual field then we do not see the eye. 'And there is nothing in the *visual field* that allows us to infer that it is seen by an eye' (T 5.633).

My visual space has, however, a form. In respect to length it is constructed differently than in respect to breadth, and I myself also always find myself in a definite point of my visual space so that I could ask myself whether the form of my visual space does not come from me. In a certain lateral, or better said, dorsal manner, I could bump up against myself as subject. But in spite of this I do not see myself as a subject. There does not exist in my world any knowing subject. 'In spite of this it is true that I do not see the subject. It is true that the knowing subject is not in the world, that there is no knowing subject' (NB, p. 86).

I see objects; I do not see objects as known, posited, or imagined by a subject, but rather I see them immediately. I also do not find anywhere a subject who knows the objects through the *fact* that it knows them.

31 The use of the word 'I' can often lead us into error. If I say that I perceive a perceiving I, then I am in error, that is to

say, I then confuse the I with an object in the world. 'One of the most deceptive descriptive methods of our language is the use of the word "I", especially where it represents the immediate experience, as in "I see a red speck"' (PR 57). The seeing of the red speck is, of course, immediate. To it there does not belong any seeing I. If I now just say, 'I perceive x', and x is here supposed to represent a physical object, then I falsely set up a relation between two worldly objects, between the, so to speak, perceiving I and the perceived x. (Here there can be no talk of perceiving in the immediate sense.) (See PR 57.) Words such as 'observe', 'perceive', belong to the normal 'physicalistic' language in which one deals with tables, boxes, and other physical objects (see PR 57). If one says that I perceive a perceiving I, then one speaks of the I as a box of matches.

The I is simply not an object. It is no object for precisely the reason that I cannot stand over against it. 'I stand objectively over against every object. But not the I' (NB, p. 80).

II

32 If I do not discover the I as a knowing subject, how does the I then enter philosophy? The I is a metaphysical subject, that is, not appearing as such and still able to be grasped philosophically, in that it makes itself known in the world in a twofold way. Namely: by the fact that the world is *my* world and by the fact that I am the limit, not a part, of the world (see T 5.641; NB, p. 82).

I can, to be sure, not draw the limits of my world, but the world is limited and I am myself its limit. How is that shown? In language. '*The limits of my language* means the limits of my world' (see T 5.6; see above No. 21). Everything which can be described in language is in the world. If, therefore, I could describe the limit of the world, then it would simply not be a limit. The limit of the world is not the limit of something extended. It is inherent in the world itself. Since my language means the world, the limits of my language are the limits of my world. So, therefore, language is also limited in itself. That is to say, I cannot place myself outside of language and speak about it, that is, about how it describes the world. One cannot speak about what *can* be said. One can only say it.

33   There is, therefore, no knowing subject. The metaphysical subject exists as the I about which there can be a philosophical discourse and about which the discourse is mediate. And finally there is the willing, world-altering subject as immediate subject. While we could, for example, say instead of 'I think' 'it thinks', we could not say 'it wills' but we have to say 'I will'. The I as willing, and thereby as a bearer of ethics, is the centre of my world (see NB, p. 80).

III

34   Besides the metaphysical subject as the I of philosophy and the willing, world-altering subject, there appears the I as personal I. This I is immediately conscious of itself.

Difficulties and misunderstandings result from the fact that there are two uses of the word 'I': one that means immediate consciousness and another which signifies the I.

If we signify the I, if we, as it were, point in its direction as towards an object, then we can speak here of the 'object use' of the word 'I'. If we want to bring our inner state to expression, then we are dealing with a 'subject use'. The 'I' of the object use and the subject use is not something different. The 'I' is only shown as something different with these two uses of the word 'I'.

'There are two different cases in the use of the word "I" (or "my") which I might call "the use as object" and "the use as subject". Examples of the first kind of use are these: "My arm is broken", "I have grown six inches", "I have a bump on my forehead", "The wind blows my hair about". Examples of the second kind: "*I* see so-and-so", "*I* hear so-and-so", "*I* try to lift my arm", "*I* think that it will rain", "*I* have a toothache" (. . .).

'To say: "I have pain" is no more a statement *about* a particular person than moaning is.

'The word "I" does not mean the same as "L.W.", even if I am L.W., nor does it mean the same as the expression "the person who is now speaking". But that doesn't mean that

"L.W." and "I" mean different things. All it means is that these words are different instruments in our language' (BB, pp. 66–7).

35   With the subject use of the word 'I' I do not designate a person, but myself. There are various criteria of identity of a person, but I am not using one here. If I say: 'I am in pain' then I do not want to direct attention to a definite *person*, but to *me*. (See PI 404, 405, 406.)

36   The object use of the word 'I' leads beyond the problem of the body to the philosophical problem of psychic processes and states and of behaviourism, which treats statements about states of consciousness as disguised statements about bodily behaviour or tendencies to bodily behaviour.

Actually we have already taken the first fateful, even if apparently harmless, step if we speak at all of processes and states and leave the matter undefined. For we already have an objective concept of them (see PI 308).

This matter is still alleviated through the fact that I do indeed have a body and can interchange the I with it. ' "I" means clearly my body, because *I* am in this room; and "I" is essentially something which is in a place, and in a place located in the same space in which there are also other bodies' (PR 55). We can also intend with 'I' something bodiless that has its place in the body. Precisely this bodiless thing in the body appears then to be the genuine I. 'We feel then that in the cases in which "I" is used as subject, we don't use it because we recognize a particular person by his bodily characteristics; and this creates the illusion that we use this word to refer to something bodiless, which, however, has its seat in our body. In fact *this* seems to be the real ego, the one of which it was said, "Cogito, ergo sum". – "Is there then no mind, but only body?" Answer: the word "mind" has meaning, i.e., it has a use in our language; but saying this doesn't yet say what kind of use we make of it" (BB, p. 70).

But I also objectivate the immediate I by bringing it to expression, in as much as I model the use of the word 'I' along the lines of the use of the demonstrative 'this person' or the use of 'he'. (See BB, p. 68). Instead of saying: 'I am in pain', I can also simply moan. But if I say that I am in pain then the use as subject along with the use as object can be exchanged with the form of a statement about a third person. 'The difference between the propositions "I have pain" and "he has pain" is not that of "L.W. has pain" and "Smith has pain". Rather, it corresponds to the difference between moaning and saying that someone moans' (BB, p. 68).

The immediacy of the personal I is shown also in the use of the word 'here'. The philosopher who says to himself: 'I am here', takes over from the sentence the verbal expression in that 'here' is a place in the common visual space. He thinks of the 'here' as the 'here' in visual space. The use of this sentence is only meaningful if my voice and the direction from which I am speaking are supposed to be known by another person (see BB, p. 72). That is, therefore, because I am still situated in the common visual space. If the philosopher says: 'I am here' he actually is saying something like 'here is here' (see BB, p. 72). The word 'I', therefore, does not name a person and the word 'here' does not name a place (see PI 410).

This fact shows that the I in its immediacy is in its space and in its body in such a way that neither the one nor the other can be signified as more definite and that the I can thereby be replaced by a description (see BB, p. 74).

37   But with every case of immediacy I can, to be sure, observe myself. Instead of simply saying: 'I am conscious', I say: 'I observe' or: 'I perceive that I am conscious.' The sentence then does not actually say that I am conscious, but that my attention is focused in such and such a fashion.

Now a difficulty arises from the fact that I can observe again my observing, that I can direct my attention to my attention itself. We may not, then, exchange the observing for the observed, the attending for that which it is directed towards. I observe what is observed immediately. Simultaneously there arises a state of the observing which I can once again observe.

'If you observe your own grief, which senses do you use to observe it? A particular sense; one that *feels* grief? Then do you feel it *differently* when you are observing it? And what is the grief that you are observing – is it one which is there only while it is being observed?

' "Observing" does not produce what is observed. (That is a conceptual statement.)

'Again: I do not "observe" what only comes into being through observation. The object of observation is something *else*' (PI, p. 187).

What results from confusing what is observed with the process of observing we see from the case of introspection, with which William James concluded that the 'self' consists principally of 'peculiar motions' in the head and between the head and throat. James in no way shows the meaning of the word 'self' or similar words such as 'person', 'man', 'himself', 'I myself'; what he showed was rather the state of attending of a philosopher who says the word 'self' to himself, and who then wants to analyse the meaning of this state of attending. (See PI 413.)

D

THE DOUBLING OF REALITY

I

38 Between the world and the I there is effected a constant doubling which appears to start from things and leads ever further in various stages. Finally one arrives at a doubling which appears to be accomplished by the I.

39 First and foremost and always we so repose in things, are so immediately alongside of them, that it is they themselves who say themselves. They say themselves and this self-saying is just like an original, scarcely distinguishable doubling of themselves.

Often when we stand before flowers or before a beautiful colour pattern, we feel ourselves 'addressed'. We also give expression to this feeling and say: 'that says something to me.' But what it says is not an indication, nor a message. It does not say something else; it says itself. 'A friend and I once looked at beds of pansies. Each bed showed a different kind. We were impressed by each in turn. Speaking about them my friend said: "What a variety of colour patterns, and each says something." And this was just what I myself wished to say.

'Compare such a statement with this: "Every one of these men says something" –

'If one had asked what the colour pattern of the pansy said, the right answer would have seemed to be that it said itself' (BB, p. 178).

If I turn my attention to a colour and allow myself to be absorbed by it, it is as if the colour says itself, describes itself. 'It seems as though the colour which I see was its own description' (BB, p. 175). Normally a picture is something that illustrates something. 'We make ourselves a picture of. . .' In the cases described it is to a certain degree the fact itself – that such and such is the case – which is a picture of itself.

I would also like to say about a (correct) picture that it says itself to me. That it says something resides in itself, in its own structures, in its forms and colours.

40   The expression 'it says something to me' can also be meant more explicitly: it tells me something, it tells me itself, just as a story tells itself.

That it says something to me does not reside, however, in its making an impression on me, or evoking in me a certain experience. If, for example, something says something to me, then it uses words to some extent, it is embedded in language. Being-spoken-to, 'letting something say something to one', 'letting something be told to one' is no inner experience but rather the immediate grasp of what – supported by a whole system, that is, by language – is expressed in a language (see PG 121). It is important here to see that something is set off immediately from itself, and this is so in a system which, as a system, does not first appear and is expressed in this self-contrasting.

41   In self-saying there is found a first, not really accomplished, doubling of things with themselves. This first doubling is also shown in the identity of a thing with itself (see PI 215). The paradigm of identity is the case of something well-known. If something is well-known to me, then I see it as the same thing which I already know. But I do not compare it to a picture of itself, I see it precisely as the same, the completely known. It coincides with itself. What is compared immediately with itself in the case of something's being totally known is one thing and not two: 'Familiarity confirms an appearance without, however, comparing it with something else. It labels it, as it were. . . . It is like saying: this motion goes as easily as if it had been practised. . . . And it is not so much that I compare the object with a picture that stands beside it, but rather the object *coincided* with itself. I see, therefore, only one thing and not two' (PG 119).

The identity of something with itself means that the thing fits together into itself, into its own forms and structures.

'"A thing is identical with itself." There is no finer example of a useless proposition, which yet is connected with a certain play of the imagination. It is as if in imagination we put a thing into its shape and saw that it fitted.

'We might also say: "Everything fits into itself." Or again: "Everything fits into its own shape." At the same time we look at a thing and imagine that there was a blank left for it, and that now it fits into it exactly.

'Does this spot "*fit*" into its white surrounding? – *But that is just how it would look* if there had at first been a hole in its place and it then fitted into the hole. But when we say "it fits" we are not simply describing this appearance; not simply this *situation*.

' "Every coloured patch fits exactly into its surrounding" is a rather specialized form of the law of identity' (PI 216).

In the apparent uselessness of the proposition about the identity of a thing with itself is shown its original doubling.

If we speak about the familiarity of a thing, that is not quite as if we were to compare what is seen with an original image of itself. It is rather like the feeling we have if an object slides into a box without resistance that fits it, which is also the case if no box that fits it is at all available. We could therefore imagine every object in an invisible box. The thing is not recognized as itself, but it is itself, although not yet really comparable nor, in fact, compared. It is not interpreted; I rest in it.

It does not happen that here there is nothing more to be interpreted: 'rather: I do not interpret. I do not interpret because I feel at home in the present picture. If I do interpret then I go along the path of thought from level to level' (Z 234; see PG 99).

II

42   A first step in disengaging from a state of resting in the things themselves occurs in the process of drawing. I draw something to get to know it better. 'Just as one learns to see a face better if one draws it' (Z 255). In this process of drawing there is made known for the first time the possibility of agreement, of the primordial relation between the thing as drawn and what is being drawn. Agreement on the basis of doubling is itself presupposed (see Z 348). If there were no such thing as

D

doubling and agreement, then there would be no language, nothing at all (see z 351).

III

43   The process of disengaging from resting in things is continued beyond the doubling-drawing into the that-determination. If, for example, I look at a flower, then I double it with itself without making a statement. If I make reference to a fact, that always means: to make reference to the fact that. . .'To make reference to a fact means to assert something, to make a statement' (PG, p. 200).

IV

44   While in letting things say themselves, we rest in them, while we let things say themselves . . . and while yet even in the establishing of facts we meet with a doubling which to some extent arises from the things themselves, in the process of intending we go from ourselves towards things. We do not thereby have a dead image of something, but we are dealing with a living movement towards what is intended (see PG 107; PI 455–6; PG 98; PG 109).

The difficulty here is that intending indeed is a conscious process and meaning or intending cannot be only a process *within* consciousness, for it means, indeed, *something*. As long as we simply treat meaning or intending (*das Meinen*) as an inner processs which contains a faithful picture of what it means, it cannot mean at all. It is something dead, isolated. Of itself it has to point to something, be related to something. And it also must do this not point-by-point and in an isolated manner, for then this relatedness could be interpreted in various ways, but by standing in a living relationship, which is embedded in a living system, to what it intends. Therefore, not only is something intended but this something is only this something in pointing beyond itself – towards a living systematic context in which it is this something. 'If I try to describe the process of intention, I feel first and foremost that it can do what it is supposed to only by containing an extremely faithful picture of what it intends. But further, that that too does not go far enough, because a picture, whatever it may be, can be variously interpreted; hence this picture too in its turn stands isolated. When one has the picture in view by itself it is suddenly dead, and it is as if something had been taken away from it, which had given it life. It is not a thought, not an intention; whatever accompaniments we imagine for it, articulate or inarticulate processes, or any feeling whatsoever, it remains isolated, it does not point outside itself to a reality beyond. . . . And now it seems to us as if intending could not be any process at all, of any kind whatsoever. – For what we are dissatisfied with here is the grammar of *process*, not the specific kind of process. – It could be said: we should call any process "dead" in this sense' (PG 100).

If in the case of intending we imagine a process then there arises a twofold problem. First, the process appears as something dead, because precisely as a process it is now something isolated, something within my consciousness. In itself a word, or a sign, or a process is dead. Only in the living process of meaning is the word, the sign, the image living. If we step outside of this (process) of meaning then the sign or the sentence appears to us as a lifeless, trivial thing. A sentence without a sense which besouls it is a dead thing. What gives it its life is the use which is made of it in living meaning (see BB, p. 4). If, for example, in a brightly illuminated cinema we let the film unroll slowly picture by picture, then we would have something like isolated, dead processes, which indeed present images but mean or intend nothing. If the light is extinguished and the film proceeds and we let ourselves be absorbed by it, then we live in it, then we have a picture of what liveliness of meaning means as opposed to dead processes. 'Let us imagine we are sitting in a darkened cinema and are living in the happenings in the film. The room is now illuminated, but the film continues on the screen. But suddenly we see it "from outside" as movements of light and dark patches on a screen' (PG 98).

But wherein does the sign, the image, the sentence have its life? It is language! Language is not present as such. Rather it is the net of living references which we have at our disposal and in which the sentence has its sense (see PG 101, 102).

That we use a sentence means, that is to say, that we understand a language.

The sign (the sentence) gets its significance from the system of signs, from the language to which it belongs. Roughly: understanding a sentence means understanding a language.

'As a part of the system of language, one may say, the sentence has life' (BB, p. 5).

The second question which is asked after the one dealing with the problem of isolation, of the 'dead' process, is: how is the intending process, this process in my consciousness, related to the intender?

V

45   We first of all represent this process to ourselves as a sort of shadow of reality. The idea of a shadow has several sources. One of them is the twofold use of a sentence in which I state that I am thinking about something. We say: 'I am thinking the same thing as he is.' Then thinking appears to have an object present. And we say: 'I am expecting him.' Then thinking appears to have a nonpresent object. The question then arises: how can we expect something that is not the case? The solution then seems to be that instead of a fact we have to represent to ourselves a shadow, as it were something which comes as close as possible to the fact but without itself being it. How do we arrive at such an idea as a shadow? Well we can indeed establish that two sentences taken from different languages have the same meaning. We can then be inclined to distinguish between sense and sentence and to succumb to the temptation of making sense into a shadow entity. 'And we argue: "therefore, the sense is not the same as the sentence", and ask the question: "What is the sense?" And we make of "it" a shadowy being, one of the many which we create when we wish to give meaning to substantives to which no material objects correspond' (BB, p. 36).

A further source of the idea that a shadow is the object of our thoughts consists in the following. Normally we interpret a picture: we translate it into another kind of picture in order to understand it.

We can now imagine that the shadow is a picture that is so

connected with its object that we cannot ask what kind of intention it has: that is to say, the fact itself whose shadow it is (see BB, p. 36). The shadow then is a kind of picture that is very similar to a representational picture. That is, it is a picture 'the intention of which *cannot be questioned* . . . but which we understand without interpreting it' (BB, p. 36). It is a kind of copy, a picture by reason of similarity. If we think of a description as a kind of word picture, as a copy which resembles an original, as pictures which hang on the wall and directly portray how something looks and is constituted, then there is something misleading about this (see PI 291; BB, p. 37). We can imagine a picture which, although it is correct, has no resemblance to its object. A sentence is just such a picture. But if we take a close look at this possibility, then we also no longer need to insert a shadow between sentence and reality. 'For now the sentence itself can serve as such a shadow. The sentence is just such a picture, which hasn't the slightest similarity with what it represents' (BB, p. 37). In the sentence words and things are joined together without a shadow having been shoved between them.

46 We have to give up, therefore, the notion of a shadow between sentence and reality. The notion that what we intend, what we wish, what we expect, has to be present as a shadow *in* our meaning or wishing, is rooted in our forms of expression. Then it is completely correct to say: the mere shadow is not sufficient, for it stops in front of the object, and we want the intending or the wish to contain the object itself. The confusion arises from the facts which we mean or which we wish not yet being here. We imagine that every clarification of what we wish or intend is somewhat inferior to the explanation which shows us a real fact and that it is, so to speak, only its shadow. That is naturally an error, for after the wish has been fulfilled I need give no better explanation of it than what I wished before: namely the fact itself.

To intend something, to wish something, to expect something, is no process occurring within consciousness which still would have to be somehow put in connection with something outside of consciousness. When I intend something I find myself immediately related to what I intend. Moreover, what is intended, or wished for, or expected, in no way needs to be present.

I do not need to be able to point to it. Indeed, intending is not a pointing to anything at all: ' "To intend him" says something like: to speak of him. Not: to point to him. And if I speak *of him*, there exists surely a connection between my speech and the thing itself, but this connection consists in the application of the discourse, not in an act of pointing' (z 24; see z 18, 19, 20). "That you meant 'playing the piano' consisted in your *thinking* about playing the piano."

'That in this letter you meant with the word "you" this man consisted in your writing to *him*.

'The mistake is saying that intending consists in something' (z 16).

Intending does not consist in something, but it is completely simple and immediate: intending what I intend. Actually the difficulty which comes up here appears more encompassing and deeper. It lies in our asking quite universally how reality in general – whether we now intended it or grasp it in some other way – enters into our thoughts and into our head. We falsely make out of our meaning and out of what we mean two realities independent of one another, that is, out of our thinking and out of the objects about which we think. 'Our difficulty can be put this way: We think about things, – about Mr Smith; but Mr Smith need not be present' (BB, p. 38). But there is nothing mysterious here. No strange spiritual act is performed here which in some way conjures up Mr Smith in our minds, but to intend Mr Smith, that is the connection itself (see BB, pp. 37ff). The relation between our thoughts and reality is immediate.

The objects we think about are just as little *in* the head as they are *in* the thoughts (see PG 96).

'How does the thought manage to represent? – The answer could be: "Don't you really know? You certainly see it if you think." There is simply nothing hidden.

'How does the sentence do it? There is nothing concealed' (PG 63).

If the thought represents something, if the sentence represents something, then we cannot and need no more ask: how then does it happen? How does the thought or sentence represent something? It simply does it. There is nothing more to be sought. It is an ultimate.

VI

47   By meaning or intending we move towards things. At first
it appeared as if we had a double picture, a shadow, a copy of
what we intend, in our consciousness. That is certainly not the
case, as we saw, but in intending, wishing, expecting, and so on,
we are more active than when it is things which express themselves to some extent to us *by themselves* (*von sich aus*).

Let us now return once again to the case of factual determination in which we duplicate reality with itself by giving expression to it.

With the determination of a fact we make an utterance, we
express something, we come to an understanding about something. What we utter, that by means of which we come to an
understanding, we call a sentence. The sentence is therefore not
merely the expression of a thought, but the means of coming to
understand. 'Misleading parallel: the cry, an expression of pain
– the sentence, an expression of a thought!

'As if the goal of a sentence were to let one know how the
other person feels: only, that is to say, in the thought apparatus
and not in the stomach' (PI 317). The sentence is not expression
of an inner feeling but expression of a sense.

A sentence is composed of words: a word has a meaning, a
sentence has a sense. We will see later what is involved with
the meaning of a word. But we now can already say that a word
has to be explained to us so that we can understand it (see w,
p. 237). Because the sentence has a sense we can explain with
sentences the meanings of words.

'The meanings of simple signs (words) must be explained to
us if we are to understand them.

'With propositions, however, we make ourselves understood'
(T 4.026).

VII

48   The sentence is essentially something which has sense.
If the sentence has *sense* then it has to show its sense (see PI
500). The sense cannot be exhibited once again by another
sentence. What can be said is said *by* a sentence. That it is said

by means of this sentence is shown in the sentence itself; it cannot again be said by means of another sentence. The sentence that the cat is lying on the carpet has the sense that the cat is lying on the carpet. It shows this sense, which itself cannot be said by another sentence (see T 4.022).

That the sense of a sentence is shown in the sentence itself and is not exhibited by means of another sentence one can also see by the fact that the comprehension of all sentences and, therefore, of each and every sentence cannot be expressed by means of a sentence. 'What can be said can be said to me through a sentence; therefore nothing that is necessary for the comprehension of *all* sentences can be said' (NB, p. 25).

49 Yet is not what is essential about a sentence its sense? Does it not have the general form: 'such and such is the case' or 'the facts are such and such'? If we say: 'such and such is the case' then this can be true or false. We could, therefore, also say: a sentence is everything which can be true or false. So it now seems that, therefore, that which the concept 'true' fits is a sentence (see PI 136). Therefore, a sentence would not be what has sense, but what can be true or false.

Still, we have to be able to understand a sentence, that is, grasp its sense without also knowing whether it is true or false (see NB, p. 93). The truth or falsity of a sentence does not consist in its having a sense, that is, a *definite* relation to reality, but in its *having* one (see NB, p. 24).

But that must not lead us to overlook that the question of the 'such and such' in 'such and such is the case' precedes the question of truth. The question of sense precedes the question of truth, and sense is independent of truth (see T 4.063). 'Whether an utterance has a sense can never be a question of experience. For experience teaches only whether the sentence is true or false. But in order to determine whether the sentence is true or false I must have already given it a sense.

'Therefore, whether a sentence has a sense cannot ever depend on whether it is true' (w, p. 244; see NB, p. 24).

50 'True' and 'False' are not, to be sure, chance properties of a sentence, but to its sense there belongs the possibility of being true or false (see NB, p. 108).

But what does it mean to say: to discover that an expression has a meaning? How can I then not only utter a meaningful sentence, but also intend it, if not through a relation to reality? (See PI 511.) For do not sense and truth collapse together? Do they not stand and fall with one another? (See z 131.) 'And is it not as if you wanted to say: "if things were not such and such then there is no sense in saying that they are"?' (z 132.)

VIII

51   The distinction between sense and truth is rooted in the accomplished doubling and reality. Between doubled reality and reality itself there exists an agreement. Instead of agreement we could also simply say: pictorial character (see PG, p. 212).

We then have to explain what we call a picture of something (see PG 113). For that purpose the method of picturing has to be definite. For only then can we compare reality with the proposition which pictured it. Only then can we see whether it is true or false. 'Whether a sentence is *true* or *false* must be shown. But we have to know beforehand *how* it will be shown' (NB, p. 23).

That a sentence is true or false means that it is possible to decide whether it is true or false. But the problem is: what does the ground for such a decision look like? (see oc 200.) The ground for decision is contained in some way in this sentence itself. 'In order to be able to make a statement at all we have to know – in a sense – how things are if the statement is true (and this is precisely what we portray).

'The proposition *expresses* what I do not know, but what, however, I have to know in order to be able to utter it at all. That is what I *show in it*' (NB, p. 18). I am immediately connected with reality and reality lets itself be expressed and pictured by me. On the basis of this connection with reality I know when the portrayal is in agreement with reality and when the expression has succeeded. The connectedness and the possibility of comparing support the possibility of the sentence. Therefore, the possibility is shown in it.

52   The proposition pictures reality. It thereby distinguishes

itself from reality. If A is supposed to be a picture of B, then it may neither completely resemble B, for otherwise it would be B itself and not a picture of B, nor may it be completely unlike B. There has to be something in common between the picture and what is being pictured so that the picture can at all be a picture of what it is portraying (see T 2.161). This common element is the 'form', the 'logical form', or also the 'form of picturing' (see T 2.18). This form is not something which can be derived from, abstracted from, and expressed by the two of them. The common form *shows* itself. The picture is connected with reality, it reaches out to it, it touches it (see T 2.1511, 2.1515). It is reality itself which shows, expresses, says itself in the picture.

In picturing reality we create as it were a doubled reality: one represents the other and therefore becomes itself a reality, which, however, is related to the other, and is connected with it. We can move about in representations as in a kind of reality. We are thereby related by means of the picture to reality, even if we should forget it.

If I set off reality from itself, form a picture of it and represent it, then I do this in a certain way and manner. I call this the method of picturing or the method of representation. For example, a melody that is repeated in notes is a picture of the melody. That I choose for this picturing a definite method, definite written signs and their spatial ordering, that is the picture itself. It is the method of representation whose result is the picture.

It is not, however, the manner of representation itself which pictures. Only the proposition is a picture. The manner of representation, the method of representation, the method of picturing, have, however, to be determined, before I compare reality with the proposition. In the proposition reality is, in a certain way, compared with itself! And the method of this comparing has to be given to me before I can compare in return (see NB, p. 23). 'The proposition has to indicate to us through its sense how we are supposed to be convinced of its truth or falsity' (PR 148). It has to show how it could be proved. What does the manner of representation do? It determines *how* reality is to be compared with the picture (see NB, p. 22). A confusion lies close to hand here: between the relation of the manner of representation of a proposition to its sense and of the proposition's relation to truth (see NB, p. 22). The truth relation is the same for all propositions, but the manner of representation is at times different.

53 How a proposition pictures is shown to us also when we consider proof and verification. For: 'Proof is not the vehicle for arriving at any place at all, but the very thing itself' (W, p. 109). On the other hand one can only prove a proposition after whose truth one can inquire (see PR 167). However, in order to be able to inquire after its truth, we have to have previously given a sense to the proposition. The sense is unfolded in the process of verification. 'Verification is not *an* index of truth, but *the* sense of the sentence. (Einstein: what a quantity is is how it is measured.)' (PR 166.) The sense of a proposition is the method of verification. This is, therefore, not the means of establishing the truth of a proposition, but it is the sense itself (see W, p. 47). In this respect it makes it possible to decide whether the proposition is true or false. One has to know the verification in order to understand the proposition at all. To give the verification is to unfold the sense of the proposition. Therefore, one cannot also look for a method of verification. For the method is only shown in the fact that through it what the proposition says is established (see W, p. 227). 'The question about the kind and possibility of verification of a sentence is only a special form of the question: "how do you mean that"' (PI 353). That also means that I have different meanings if I come upon different verifications (see W, p. 53). The self-showing of the connection between sense and truth, between sentence and reality, is completed in the proof. To be able to prove something is: to prove it (see PR 167; PR 165).

IX

54 Why do we say: 'Reality is compared with the sentence', and not: 'The sentence is compared with reality'? (See T 4.05.) Why does the sentence appear to us as placed as a judge before reality? Why does reality seem to demand to be compared with it? (See PG 85.)

The reason is that how reality is represented to us depends on our manner of representation. The reason is that reality, if it shows itself, shows itself only in the sentence, in language.

What symbols in particular there are with which we mean reality, which sentence we form, this depends on our creative activity (see T 5.555–6).

In forming a sentence we construct a perspective within which this sentence gets its sense. There is no isolated sentence. It is embedded in a system which we create with our representation. This system in its own way determines how we see reality and what distinctions we make in it. If what is common to sentence and reality is the logical form, the system which the sentence determines is the logical space. Logical space is what is common to a sentence-system and reality.

A sentence, or rather a sentence-system, determines a logical space, sets it up as it were. It lets us systematically see and grasp reality in this or that fashion. 'If I describe a part of the visual field, then my description has to still contain the whole visual field. The form (the logical form) of the speck presupposes as a matter of fact the whole space' (PR 88). The sentence determines a logical place (see NB, p. 24). At the same time it has to thoroughly encompass the whole logical space (see NB, p. 36). Accordingly it belongs to the system which determines this space and itself thoroughly encompasses the whole space. A sentence about a colour thoroughly encompasses the colour space (see W, pp. 76ff).

55   An example of the determination of a logical space is the activity of measuring. Spatial measuring constructs first of all a space that is measurable. It lets us grasp the space as measurable. Therefore, the method of measuring is related to a definite measurement precisely as the sense of a sentence is related to its truth or falsity. The activity of measuring presupposes neither a definite quantity of the object to be measured nor a definite unit of the standard measure. It creates it, as it were, in making the activity of measuring meaningful. In that I apply the method of measuring, space is defined as measurable and a yardstick is established. 'All that I need is: I have to be able to be certain that I can apply a yardstick.

'If I therefore say: "three steps more and I will see red", that presupposes that I in any case can apply yardsticks of length and colour' (PR 44).

The example of measuring shows us how we apply to reality a whole system of sentences as a yardstick. 'A *sentence-system* is laid up against reality like a yardstick. I mean by that the following: if I place a measure up against a spatial object I place at the same time *all the marks on the stick* up against it. Not the single divisions are placed against it, but the whole scale. If I know that the object reaches as far as division number 10, then I also know immediately that it does not reach to number 11 and 12, etc. The statements which describe to me the length of an object form a system, a sentence-system. Such a total sentence-system is compared with reality, not a single individual sentence. If, for example, I say that this or that point in the visual field is *blue*, I know not only that, but also that the point is not green, nor red, nor yellow, etc. I have applied the whole *colour-scale* at one time' (PR, p. 317; see W, p. 64).

Because all sentences belong together in this system, if one measures with one of them, then one measures at the same time with all the others. And if *one* measure is correct that excludes automatically all others (see PR 82).

X

56 That I can place a system of sentences as a measure up against reality lets us understand the remarkable dualism of positive and negative facts, and of positive and negative statements. If positive statements are made about a thing, all negative statements which touch upon the same logical space are also implicitly made along with them (see NB, p. 33). If a table is two metres long then it is not three metres long and also not one metre. Even if there follows from the sentence 'the table is two metres long' the negation of all sentences which ascribe to the table another length, all these negative sentences are not nevertheless also thought of. The negation of a sentence which ascribes another length to the table only then follows from the sentence 'the table is two metres long', if it is confronted with it (see PG, pp. 250f).

Negation points toward the logical space in which what is

negated stands and it helps us to determine its logical place.
'This man is two metres tall.' 'No he is not.' 'How tall is he
then?' If I deny that a man is two metres tall, then I say at the
same time that he has to have a height which I can determine.

Only both together, the negation and the negated proposition,
show us the sense of the whole proposition (see NB, p. 94).
One has the feeling as if one had first to make the negated
proposition true, because one would like to ask: what is not the
case? But in a negation it is not possible to first make the
negated proposition true (see PB 41). 'Only a finished proposition can be negated (. . .). Negation refers to the *finished* sense
of the negated proposition and not to its way of presenting (. . .).

'If a picture represents what-is-not-the-case in the fore-
mentioned way, this only happens through its presenting *that*
which *is* not the case.

'For the picture says, as it were: "*This* is how it is *not*", and
to the question: "*How* is it not" just the positive proposition is
the answer.

'It might be said: The negation refers to the very logical place
which is determined by the negated proposition (. . .).

'The negating proposition determines a *different* logical place
from the negated proposition.

'The negated proposition not only draws the boundary
between the negated domain and the rest; it actually points to
the negated domain.

'The negating proposition uses the logical place of the
negated proposition to determine its logical place. By describing
the latter as the place that is outside the former' (NB, pp. 25–6).

Let us see what that looks like concretely: 'This man is two
metres tall.' 'No, he is not.' 'He is also not *over* two metres tall,
nor *under* one metre sixty.' 'The man therefore has a height.
And this height lies between two metres and one metre sixty.'

Negation in arithmetic has to have a different meaning than
in customary linguistic usage. Otherwise I would have to be
able to form a picture of how it would be true if $2 \times 2 = 5$ were
true, if I, that is, were to establish that $2 \times 2 = 5$. And I can also
not imagine how 7 is divisible by 3 if I say that 7 is not divisible
by 3. 'All that follows as a matter of course from the fact that
mathematical equations are not propositions' (PR 200; see PR,
p. 203).

XI

57 If I construct a system of propositions with which I want to determine and grasp reality, then I follow rules, rules governing the manner of representation. The boundary-stakes of these rules are tautology and contradiction. Tautology and contradiction have the external form of propositions. While the proposition shows what it says, tautology and contradiction show nothing at all. Tautology represents nothing and a contradiction can represent nothing (see NB, p. 24). Tautology and contradiction are senseless, because through them I cannot bring the proposition up to the point where its truth or falsity can be decided (see T 4.461). In the one case it is already true unconditionally and in the other case it cannot be true. 'Tautologies and contradictions are not, however, nonsensical. They are part of the symbolism, just as "O" is part of the symbolism of arithmetic' (T 4.4611). That is, every time I arrive at 'O' I have to begin anew in a certain way.

Tautology and contradiction are not, however, two null-points in the scale of propositions. They are opposed poles. In this sense they do not say nothing but say where a proposition is located: namely between them (see NB, p. 45).

58 A tautology is no rule and we do not let a contradiction function as a rule. If we want to represent reality why do we fear a contradiction more than a tautology (see Z 689)? Because we do not get entangled in a tautology, and if we did in fact do so, it would be without meaning, since it is true unconditionally. Besides, we can use a tautology in a certain sense. 'What characterizes the application of a tautology is that we never use a tautology itself in order to express something with this propositional form but that we avail ourselves of it only as a method in order by means of it to make visible logical relations between other statements.

'If we were blind the telescope would not be able to make us see; should language not already show everything logical, then tautology would also not be able to teach us anything.

'*To the method of tautology there corresponds in mathematics the proof of an equation.* The same factor used in the case of tautologies – namely, the making visible of the agreement of two structures – is also utilized in the proof of an equation. If we prove a numerical calculation we transform the two sides until their equality is *shown*. That is, in fact, the same procedure on which the use of tautologies rests.

'*Something* in this conception is therefore correct. *The equation is no tautology.* Rather the *proof of the equation* rests on the same principle on which the application of a tautology rests.

'It is common to mathematics and to logic that the proof is no proposition but that the proof *demonstrates* something' (W, p. 219).

After having briefly touched upon the one boundary-mark of rules, tautology, let us turn to the other one, contradiction. I do not allow a contradiction to function as a rule. Now what happens if I discover a contradiction amidst my rules? With this I discover that they are no rules at all and look for new ones. 'What is a rule? If I, for example, say: "do that and don't do it!" the other person does not know what he is to do: that is, we do not allow a contradiction to function as a rule. We call precisely a contradiction not a rule – or more simply: the grammar of the word "rule" is such that a contradiction is not characterized as a rule. If, now, a contradiction appears among my rules, I would say: those are not rules in the sense in which I otherwise speak of rules. What do we do in such a case? Nothing is simpler: we give a new rule and thereby the matter is settled' (PR, pp. 344f; see PR, p. 322; W, pp. 124f).

59 We are afraid that if we have arrived at a contradiction everything which we have done up to that point is false. That either the starting points in the game, or the rules in accordance with which it was being played, are false. We accordingly often have the notion that a contradiction which no one has seen could be hidden in the starting points or in the rules. 'Just as with tuberculosis: one suspects nothing and one day one is dead. So one also thinks: one day the hidden contradiction could perhaps appear and then the catastrophe is at hand' (W, p. 120). Now, with a contradiction in the starting points (configurations

in the calculus or axioms) we cannot connect any meaning (see
w, p. 119; PR, p. 318; w, p. 124). A contradiction can only
appear in the true-false game, only where we make assertions:
therefore, only in the rules, in the directions for the game (see
PR, p. 321). And to ask whether the conclusions which I draw
from the starting points, and the rules which I am following,
could once lead to a contradiction also does not make any
sense as long as the contradiction is simply not there. 'I can
play as long as I can play, and everything is in order' (w, p. 120).
As long as I can play the rules are in order. They are only then
no longer in order if I *notice* that they are not. And how do I
notice that? By not being able to apply any more the rules in
use up to now (see PR, pp. 321f).

The question is: what happens now if a contradiction appears
in our rules?

The problem is, therefore, not what we have to do in order to
avoid contradiction, for we simply do not see it beforehand.
Rather: what are we supposed to do if we arrive at a contradiction (see z 688, 689)? 'A contradiction is not to be understood as a catastrophe but as a wall which indicates to us we
can go no further here' (z 687). Then we just have to look for
another way.

Let us imagine a rule for a game which says that the white
stone has to move over the black stone. If now the black stone
stands at the edge of the board the rule breaks down. I no longer
know what I have to do. How can I remove the contradiction
here? By introducing a new rule (see PR, p. 321; w, pp. 124f).
Or: 'Two rules can contradict one another. Think for example
of the case of a game of chess where a rule would run: under
such and such conditions the appropriate piece has to be taken.
But another rule would say: a knight may never be taken. If
now the appropriate piece is precisely a knight then the rules
contradict one another; I do not know what I am to do. What
do we do in such a case? Very simple: we introduce a new rule
and with that the conflict is resolved' (w, p. 120).

To develop a proof for freedom from contradiction could
only mean: to see through all the rules (see w, pp. 137f). In the
case of rules, however, if we are in the process of establishing
them, they are not transparent to us. If we then follow the rules,
things can be different than we had imagined. And then we have

E

to try to find out where we are caught up in our rules, that is, where we have to replace rules (see PI 125).

'The contradiction can only be hidden in the sense that it is, as it were, hidden higgledy-piggledy in the rules, in the un-ordered part of the grammar; but there it does not do anything, since it is to be removed through setting the grammar in order.

'Why may rules not contradict one another? Because other-wise there would be no rules' (PG, p. 305; see RFM II-84).

XII

60   The active process of separating proper to the doubling of reality leads from the 'immediately aproaching something in intending' over the 'that-establishment' to the assertion, to the proposition, to a system of propositions. Now, as we already saw it adumbrated in the process of intending and expecting, the process of separating can reach such a point that we think of something, make ourselves a picture of something, which does not exist at all. 'These [difficulties] can all be summed up in the question: "how can one think what is not the case?" ' (BB, p. 30). This is, besides, a beautiful example of a philosophical question. For while this question bewilders us we nevertheless know that we often enough *do think* what is not the case. We have to discard, therefore, this – to us – fascinating and misleading manner of expression.

61   That something is not the case can mean that I am in error. But I can be in error only within an existing pre-given system. About the system itself I cannot be in error. 'If I think that King's College is on fire when it is not on fire, the fact of its being on fire does not exist. Then how can I think it? How can we have a thief who does not exist? Our answer could be put in this form: I can't hang him when he doesn't exist' (BB, p. 31). Even if there is no thief there is still a space in which there is such a thing as a thief and in which I can look for him. And I am bound to this space.

In space one has a relation to a place where one is not (PR 43). Remembrance and reality, representation and reality, are in *one* space (see PR 38). All that is part of our language and is contained in our language.

62   That something is not the case can also mean that something is not before me, is not bodily present, if I think about it. As, for example, I can think about my brother in America (see LC, pp. 66ff). I then form for myself a picture of the absent one, who indeed exists in reality. This reality is also for me a latent background of reality. I am always indeed connected with reality. What makes this picture into an image, what connects it with reality? It is the *intention*. It is not the similarity which makes the picture into a portrait but the intention: what *he* is supposed to be (see PG 62; see BB, p. 32). The picture, the proposition, the representation *are supposed* to present reality. And that is just what is possible, because reality already exists and I already find myself in it.

The doubling detachment is accomplished, therefore, still further in the picture and in the representation.

XIII

63   While the proposition is an immediate 'picture' in which reality is shown and through which reality is presented, a genuine picture is only a mediate representation. How is this picture connected with reality? Through my understanding that it *says* something to me. In understanding I go through the picture to reality (see PG 114).

64   I can also intentionally double reality by trying to *re*present to myself something which is not real as if it were real. This is not an attempt taking place in representing but an attempt to represent. 'If, for example, someone asks me: "How do you greet N, how do you go up to him?", in order to be able to answer, I can imagine N's coming in the door and I make, say, a movement of greeting' (*Eine Philosophische Betrachtung* [Wittgenstein's reworking of the *Brown Book*], *Schriften* 5, p. 194). Here there are close connections to remembrance and to the case of the picture (see PI 301).

65	We find the strongest contrast to 'resting in things' and to things' immediately 'saying themselves' in the activity of representation in which we seek to duplicate an object completely with itself. Representation is a doubling of *this*. 'The image must be more like its object than any picture. For however like I make the picture to what it is supposed to represent, it can always be the picture of something else as well. But it is essential to the image that it is the image of *this* and of nothing else. Thus one might come to regard the image as a superlikeness' (PI 389). If we see something, something happens to us; if we imagine something, we do not observe. Representing or imagining is rather like a doing; seeing rather like a receiving.

'Difference: "endeavouring to see something" and "endeavouring to imagine something'. In the first case one says something like "look right here" and in the second case, "close your eyes!" ' (z 626) Because representing (in imaginal form) is a doing, a creative act, it excludes the presence of what is represented (see z 627–46).

66	Nevertheless, no matter how far in the doubling of reality we also detach ourselves from it, or appear to detach ourselves from it, still we always remain bound to it. That is to say, we do not in supplementary fashion connect anew with reality what has been detached, but in the 'activity of detaching' there remains a connection that goes completely through reality. This connection is manifested in the words 'able to be represented' (*vorstellbar*). For if we say that something can be represented we mean that it can exist in reality (see PI 395, 396, 397).

67	In the framework of the doubling effected by language we can, finally, proceeding beyond picture and imaginal representation (*Vorstellung*), formalize and represent reality through forms. With that the presentation of reality becomes mediate to the highest degree. 'Think now that men were accustomed always to point to objects in such a way that they described with the finger in the air, as it were, a *circle around* the object. Then one could imagine a philosopher who said: "All things are circular; for the table looks it, the stove, the lamp', etc., since he draws on each occasion a circle around the thing' (z 443).

If we represent all things by means of the same form then we do not really portray them any more. Then we make reality uniformal. The uni-formity makes reality form-less, amorphous. Logical form, that is, what picture and reality have in common, is here reduced to the barest minimum.

We pack together structures, relations, and so on, and present them merely still packed together. 'The sense of this method is to make everything amorphous and to treat them that way' (PR 170). We can apply such a method where it does not matter whether things are amorphous or not. But even then we may not forget that, in fact, the concepts with which we pack things together have their meaning through definitions with whose aid they pack (things) together in just such a way. Time and again if we want to see their connection with reality, we have to unpack the concepts which are stuck in such a form. If we do not do this, the greatest confusions can arise.

If there were only external connections, then no connection at all would be describable; there would only be oppositions. We have to develop the inner structures (see PR 26, 104).

If we formalize, we make everything amorphous. But if everything is amorphous then we cannot see meaningful structures anymore. We have made everything in-different. A formalizing description grasps reality in about the way 'in which a man carries packed in a box a mass of things which one cannot hold all in the hand. They are invisible and still we know that we are carrying them (as it were indirectly)' (PG, p. 468). The packing together gets its meaning only by means of definitions which have hidden reality in such a way. If we give in to these definitions then we uncover once again what has been hidden.

68 Sometimes we also do not notice that we have before us a packing in which something is packed that has to be unpacked. That concerns, for example, the assertion that a proposition is someone's judgement. In this case the characterization 'this proposition' is a packing which points towards a proposition which has been packed into it. A proposition must itself appear in the utterance that this proposition is someone's judgement (see NB, p. 96). Because the packing-concepts only allude to those packed-in objects, but without representing them, we let

ourselves, for example, be easily misled by the paradox of the 'Cretan Liar'. ' "The Cretan Liar". Instead of saying: "I am lying" one could also write down: "This sentence is false." The answer to this would be: "Indeed, but what sentence do you mean?" "Well now, *this* sentence." – "I understand, but about which sentence is one talking in *it*" – "This one." – "Good, and to which proposition does *this* one allude?", etc. He could not explain to us what he means in advance of the transition to a complete proposition. – One can also say: the fundamental error lies in thinking that a phrase, for example, "this sentence" can as it were allude to an object (refer from a distance) without having to represent it" (z 691). The paradox of the Cretan Liar is a warning against formalization.

E

TEMPORALITY

I

69 We move among things, portray them, represent them. By portraying and representing them we touch them and are yet separated from them. This connecting being-separated is shown not only in the spatiality of our world, in the possibility of portrayal and of language, but also in temporality. The dimension in which we touch things is in itself stretched out: distance to things and distance in itself as temporality.

70 Temporality is manifested first of all in remembrance. The fundamental question here is: 'how can one *know* that one can show it if . . .; that one can, therefore, recognize it if one sees it?' (PR 11). If I *re-cognize* (*wiedererkenne*) something, how do I know that it is what I had meant? We easily get a false concept of what happens in recognition. It seems to us as if recognition always consisted in the comparison of two impressions. As if I had a picture of an object and then recognized an object as the one which the picture represents. As if our memory preserves a picture of something seen before with which we can then compare what we now see. 'We may shed light on all these considerations if we compare what happens when we remember the face of someone who enters our room, when we recognize him as Mr So and So, – when we compare what really happens in such cases with the representation we are sometimes inclined to make of the events. For here we are often obsessed by a primitive conception, viz., that we are comparing the man we see with the memory image in our mind and we find the two to agree. I.e., we are representing "recognizing someone" as a process of identification by means of a picture (as a criminal is identified by his photo)' (BB, p. 165).

In the process of recognition, however, in fact no such comparison takes place (see PG 118). Recognition is something originary and not a comparison. 'If we should not recognize the colour green as such (due, say, to a failure of memory) we could therefore not use the word "green". But do we then have any control over this recognition so that we know that it is truly a recognition? If we speak about a recognition we mean that we know something as what it truly is, according to other criteria. "To know" means: to know what it *is*' (PG 118). *Recognition is therefore cognition.* As when I imagine a colour and then, when I have found it, recognize it. Where in that case is a comparison still possible (see PR 12)? There is found in recognition a cognition that that which is, really *is*, that is, that it is the same persisting through time. What is recognized is *shown* as the same thing that it was. I know it as what it was and now is. In recognition there is no comparison but rather what is permanent is grasped.

Furthermore, there is also a recognition which seems to us to be a recognition based on comparison. If we consider our understanding of a genre-picture we are inclined to assume that we 're'-cognize the painted men as men, the painted trees as trees. But actually there is no comparison taking place here (see PG 117). We grasp the trees and men precisely as trees and men.

71 The possibility of remembering and re-cognition is in general the possibility of being-able-to-know that something is as it is.

We do not look through our memory as through a tube into the past (see PG 118). I only know that remembrance is remembrance of the past for the reason that this belongs precisely to the essence of remembrance. The original time concept which is implied here is radically different from that of physical time (see PR 50). Re-cognition is a mental process, but one which precisely consists in my actual remembering (see PI 305, 306). Recognition itself is the only source for my knowing that something is the same.

'If I expect something to happen and then there occurs something which fulfils my expectation, does it make any sense to ask whether that is really the event which I expected? That is, how would a proposition that asserts that be verified? It is clear that the *only* source of my knowing here is the comparison of the *expression* of my expectation with what has actually happened.

'How do I know that the colour of this paper, which I call call "white", is the same as the one which I saw here yesterday? By the fact that I recognize it. And this recognition is my only source for this knowledge. Then "that it is the same" *means* that I recognize it.

'Then it is also not possible to ask whether it is probably the same and whether I am not mistaken; (whether it *is* the same and not just *appears* so)' (PR 16).

II

72   Time is, therefore, that in which sameness is given to me, namely, in difference. Sameness is generally only in difference. Only in recognition is identity shown. Recognition is, therefore, what is primary and identity is what is secondary.

73   Recognition is, therefore, not only the source of the concepts of the past and of identity, but at the same time a means of control of what is past and of identity (see PR 19). As source and control, recognition does not need a *tertium comparationis* (see PR 21).

74   These essential characteristics allow us to distinguish the memory image from the representational image. The memory image, in distinction from the representational image, has the characteristic that it is embedded in a context of the past (see BB, pp. 182f).

75   Remembrance and expectation are in immediate agreement with reality. One cannot say that the past or the future, about which memory or expectation speak, *represent* only the past or the future. I expect just as truly as I wait (see PR 35), that is, just as concretely as I concretely encounter the immediate future, expecting it and waiting only for it. In the memory image, in memory itself, no picture of the past is given to me, but the past itself.

76 Just as re-membrance shows me the same thing, a fulfilled expectation also shows me the same thing. What is strange is that the event which occurs is not distinguished from what I expected. If I say, 'I imagined it just this way', one could object: that is impossible, for a representation is one thing and reality is another, and you have put your representation in place of reality (see PG 88). The answer to this is that I can, to be sure, form a representation of what I am expecting, but that the expectation is related immediately to reality. The event (I) encounter(ed) is 'the same' one I expected (see PR 30). As immediately joined to reality expectation is the measure of itself.

'I see someone pointing a gun and say: "I expect a report." The shot is fired. – Well, that was what you expected; so did that report somehow already exist in your expectation? Or is it just that there is some other kind of agreement between your expectation and what occurred; that that noise was not contained in your expectation, and merely accidentally supervened when the expectation would not have been fulfilled; the noise fulfilled it; it was not an accompaniment of the fulfilment like a second guest accompanying the one I expected. – Was the thing about the event that was not in the expectation too an accident, an extra provided by fate? — But then what was *not* an extra? Did something of the shot already occur in my expectation? – Then what *was* extra? for wasn't I expecting the whole shot?

'The report was not so loud as I had expected. – Then was there a louder bang in your expectation' (PI 442)?

77 Because I perceive reality I do not perceive my expectation, but I expect that... The fulfilment of expectation is not something but rather an expectation that... In this way the description of expectation by means of what it expects is an internal description and not an external one (see PI 453). (An internal property or relation is one which it is unthinkable that its object does not have (see T 4.023).) In reality we do not expect the fulfilment but, for example, *that* he will come. 'The mistake is rooted in our language: we say: "I am expecting him" and: "I am expecting his arrival" and: "I am expecting that he will come"' (z 58).

78 Reality is immediate, also in time. Just as well as I know that something *is*, I know that something is that which I am expecting.

'Reality is not a property which is still missing in what is expected and which is now added if the expectation is fulfilled. – Reality is also not like the light of day which first gives colour to things if they are already there in the dark, colourless, as it were. (How do you know that you are expecting a *red* patch; that is, how do you know that a red patch is the fulfilment of what you are expecting?) But I could just as well ask: 'how do you know that it *is* a red patch?'' (PG 89; see z 60.)

III

79 To be sure, in temporality there is manifested an immediate connection with reality, but this connection is: lack, gap, being separated, dissatisfaction. The hollow space between me and the world, between me and things, is manifest in the dissatisfaction which is shown most clearly in the temporal phenomenon of expectation. However, in fact, the symbol as such appears unsatisfied in general (see PG 85). The wish, the surmise, the belief, the order, appear as something unsatisfied, something in need of completion (*Ergänzungsbedürftiges*).

But what is the paradigm from which we get the concept of dissatisfaction? Is it a hollow space, is it a feeling of hunger? But the same description that fits the empty space fits also the full space. What is lacking and what takes it away are described in the same way. And expectation is not related to its satisfaction in the way hunger is to its. Expectation is not stilled in the way hunger is (see PG 87).

The state of being unsatisfied is not being separated from what it is lacking, and yet it first makes a relation to this possible. Or, put more exactly, it *is* this relation. 'And I want to say:" the wish is unsatisfied, because it is a wish *for something*; the opinion is unsatisfied, because it is the opinion that something is the case"' (PG 85). The relation to reality itself is the state of being unsatisfied.

80	Because our relation to reality is a state of being un-satisfied, the proposition in which the relation is expressed demands satisfaction. It becomes a judicial-proposition, a judgemental-proposition, and we feel ourselves responsible for its constant satisfaction through constant comparison. 'I would like to say: "My expectation is so constituted that no matter what comes it has to agree with it or not."

'The proposition appears to us to be set up as a judge and we feel ourselves responsible before it. – It appears to demand of reality that it compare itself with it' (PG 85).

81	Expectation and the fact which satisfies it fit together. But if one wants to describe the two of them then one description is valid for both. Since the description is the same, the wish (or the expectation) and its satisfaction come into contact in language.

In language the in itself distant relation to reality is alive. Wishing does not need to show what is being wished for, it does not prefigure a picture of what is wished for in the wish-sphere (*Wunschsphäre*), but the wish is precisely a wish as expressed in language. 'Is what is wished for really there in any situation whatsoever or in any process whatsoever? – And what is our model for this situation? Is it not our language? Where then is that given which makes the wish this wish, although it yet is *only* a wish? Precisely in the wish as expressed' (PG 102). On the other hand, however, it is precisely the consideration of the linguistic expression of the wish which can awaken the appear-ance that my wish, while I wish, prefigures its fulfilment. If I say, I wish that . . . this could be confused with a shallow descrip-tion of what is wished for, a description in which what is wished for is prefigured, while in wishing I am really immediately related to what is wished for (see PG 103). What characterizes all these cases: wishes, expectations, and so on, is: we expect and wish *now*. 'It is not a later experience which decides what we are expecting. And I can say: in language expectation and fulfilment come into contact' (PG 92).

82	Everything which is expressed expresses precisely the in itself distant relation to reality. 'A wish seems already to know what will or would satisfy it; a proposition, a thought, what makes it true – even when that thing is not there at all! Whence this *determining* of what is not yet there? This despotic demand?' (PI 437.)

IV

83 Expecting and remembering are connected with looking for something. Seeking presupposes that I know what I am after, but not that what I am after also exists (see PR 28). 'I can look for him when he is not there, but not hang him when he is not there' (PI 462).

But how do I know that have found what I was looking for? I cannot compare the earlier expectation with what I encounter, for the event *replaces* the expectation. But that is precisely the answer.

But, if looking for something and expecting are replaced by what occurs, then it has to be in the same space. What is being sought for has to be in the same space with the (activity of) seeking (see PR 28). In the last analysis this space is the world itself. It is only in the world that something has meaning for me, even, and precisely, the activity of seeking. I can, therefore, only look for and expect something in the world (see PR 34).

84 The immediate connection between seeking and what is sought, between expecting and what is expected, the wish and what is wished for, is skewed for us because we judge the event the way we would the symptoms of seeking or expecting in other cases. There one element is the other person who is uneasy and paces back and forth before the door until someone comes in through the door and he is satisfied. The fundamental error consists in the comparison: the man enters – the event enters. 'As if the event were already prefigured before the door of reality and was only to enter into it (as into a room)' (PG 90; see Z 59). Expectation is internally related to what is expected. It expects *now* that what will be *will* be later. If this has occurred, the expectation is answered, to wit, by being replaced by what happens. I cannot describe the expectation along with what is fulfilled by two propositions, but only by one.

The fulfilment of the expectation is not a third thing beyond or beside expectation and its fulfilment, but it is the expectation itself which is fulfilled. *That* p will be the case is embedded in a situation, in the last analysis, in the world. Because I am already in the world I can look for individual things in it. Because the world is already *there* I can expect individual things in it.

V

85   In order to avoid misunderstandings, an hypothesis has to be distinguished from an expectation. An hypothesis is not an expectation but it produces an expectation in that it admits a confirmation in the future. 'That is, it is of the essence of an hypothesis that its confirmation is never completed. (. . .) An hypothesis is a law for the construction of propositions. One could also say: an hypothesis is a law for the forming of expectations. The probability of an hypothesis has its measure in how much evidence is necessary in order to make it advantageous to overturn it.

'Only in this sense can one say that repeated uniform experience in the past makes probable its continuation in the future' (PR 228, 229).

F

LANGUAGE

I

86 Our relation to reality is accomplished in the activity of thinking. The doubling of I and world is mirrored in the activity of thinking. Language is the vehicle of thinking. Accordingly language is the authentic medium in which world and I double one another and relate themselves to one another.

87 'When I think in language there are not 'meanings' going through my mind in addition to the verbal expressions; the language is itself the vehicle of thought' (PI 329). It sometimes seems to us that thinking is a process which accompanies speech, which perhaps could accompany also something else or run its own course independently. But with a closer look it becomes clear that thinking is not something that happens alongside, but it inheres in language (see PI 330).

Thinking and language belongs together. A child learns language in such a way that it suddenly begins to think in it. ('He suddenly begins; I mean: there is no forestage in which the child already used language, used it, so to speak, for the purpose of understanding, but did not yet think in it' (PR 5).) Does the child learn the meaning of multiplication *before* or *after* multiplying (see PG 66)? One cannot speak without thinking and one cannot think without speaking (see PI 327; PI 339, Z 101). If I think, I am speaking internally. The concept of inner speech can, however, easily mislead us, because, for a whole stretch, it parallels closely the concept of an internal process, but without coinciding with it (see PI 532f). If we want to try to treat thinking as an experience then the experience of discourse still helps us the most to approach it. Nevertheless, thinking does not really let itself be compared with other experiences. An experience is something that runs up against us, we undergo an experience passively, but thinking is something we 'do'. 'Indeed, if one speaks about an *experience* of thinking, the experience of speaking is as good as any other. But the concept of "thinking" is not a concept of experience. For one does not compare thoughts the way one compares experiences' (z 96).

88   I only call thoughts those things which have an articulate expression. An expression uses signs. In the expressive use of signs there is brought about a bond or connection with the world (see w, p. 235).

'A thought, this strange thing' (PI 428). But the thought does not occur to us as something strange or mysterious, when we think it. Any more than the sentence appears to us strange and mysterious when we say it. It only appears to us strange, then, if we treat it, so to speak, retrospectively, if we consider what we say *about* it. That is, then it appears as if the thought were in the mind and synthesized there the objects which it is thinking, as if it *contain*ed reality (see PG 105; PI 428). In doing so it is immediate living connection with reality. Behind this connection it is not possible for us to go.

The connection consists in the fact that what I am thinking is reality itself. That I can point to it in order to point out what I am thinking. And that on the basis of this bond my thoughts can be true or false. 'The agreement, the harmony, of thought and reality consists in this: if I say falsely that something is *red*, then, for all that, it isn't *red*. And when I want to explain the word "red" to someone, in the sentence: "That is not red", I do it by pointing to something red' (PI 429).

II

89   If language and thinking belong together, then language cannot be contained in thought; it cannot be found beforehand 'in the mind'. Language is in general not something *present before us* (*vorhanden*), but it is essentially latent. Our ways of talking leads us to look upon language as something on hand. ' "So you really wanted to say . . ." ' – We use this phrase in order

to lead someone from one form of expression to another. One is tempted to use the following picture: what he really "wanted to say", what he "meant" was already *present somewhere* in his mind even before he gave it expression' (PI 334).

90   Let us compare this way of speaking with what we say we are concerned with, for example, in the case of writing a letter, with finding the right expression for our thoughts. This expression compares the event to that of a translation or of a description. The thoughts are already there, or a picture or a gesture, and I am just looking for the right expression. But, 'now if it were asked: "Do you have the thought before finding the expression" what would one have to reply? And what, to the question: "What did the thought consist in, as it existed before its expression?"' (PI 335.) If I could say: 'I think without words' then I would still have to be able to express the thoughts – in words.

How do I find the right word? How do I select it from among other words? I do not always have to pass judgement or to explain, but I simply find: now it does not yet fit – and now it does. Sometimes I can say why; sometimes simply 'that is it'. 'This is simply what searching, this is what finding is like here' (PI, p. 218). That is all.

To the notion of a thinking that already exists prior to speaking there corresponds the rather current notion that it is possible not to think a proposition in the way that it is written. On the basis of this prior existing thought one would have to turn it around so that it corresponds to this thought. Or one might first think it and when one first has thought it out one can choose for it the strange manner of expression.

In the case of the notion of a pre-existing thought separated from speaking 'there is present a case, similar to the one in which someone imagines that one could not think a sentence with the remarkable word order of German or Latin just as it stands. One first has to think it, and then one arranges the words in that queer order. (A French politician once wrote that it was a peculiarity of the French language that in it words occur in the order in which one thinks them.)' (PI 336.) Thinking, however, separated from the expression of thoughts, cannot precede itself; it is not essentially another process (see PG 66). One does not think before, alongside of, or after thinking or

F

speaking. ' "Were you thinking then, as you were saying the sentence, about that, that . . ." ' – "I was only thinking what I was saying" ' (PG 66).

91   It sometimes seems to us as if we were translating out of a primitive way of thinking into our own, as if before we think there was a thought-schema at the base of our thought. Such as, say, happens if a German who speaks good English suddenly uses a Germanism. He did not first form the German expression, but it was, to some extent, there as an underlying schema (see PI 597). Indeed, there is no thinking preceding thinking itself.

92   But I already intend the total form of a sentence as soon as I begin it. Does that not then mean that it was already present in my mind before I gave expression to it? But if we say that, we construct for ourselves a misleading picture of intending. Intending is the projecting of a power (*eines Könnens*). A power is not something lying present at hand but a possibility, not a logical possibility, but a concrete possibility. Being-able-to is embedded in a situation and in human customs and institutions. 'If the technique of the game of chess did not exist, I could not intend to play a game of chess. In so far as I do intend the construction of a sentence in advance, that is made possible by the fact that I can speak the language in question' (PI 337). Language is therefore institutionalized being-able-to. One can only say something if one has learned to speak. If I want to say something, if I intend to say something, I have to be in control of the language. But in the case of intending, and in the case of wanting to speak, I do not have to speak. In willing, speaking is not yet a reality but only a possibility. But now if we think about it, we form an erroneous image of this possibility if we think of it as a concretely present potency, as a shadow entity (see RFM I-125).

The understanding (*Verständnis*) of language seems to us like a background against which the individual sentence retains its form. Still, this background is neither a process nor a state. It is: being-able-to (*Können*). If I 'can' do something, then being able to do something is also not the state which accompanies the doing. 'Being-able-to' first sees the light of day in the 'I can' as its background-possibility. 'The understanding of language, as of a game, appears like a background against which the individual sentence first gets its meaning. – But this understanding, the knowledge of language, is not a state of consciousness which accompanies the sentences of the language. Even if it (the understanding) should lead to such a state. Rather it is of the same kind as the understanding and mastery of a calculus. Therefore, like *being able* to multiply' (PG 11).

The sentence, the thought, lives in the system of language. But that does not mean that we experience the system if we use the sentence. 'But the system of language does not belong to the category of an experience. The typical experience in the case of the use of a system is not the system itself' (PG 121). In the case of being-able-to this being-able-to does not lie before us as a system. In the use of the sentence the system of language is not present as such.

And there is no need of something special to make the sentence come to life for us. In living speech the question of its being alive simply does not arise. 'If we ask on the other hand: "Why doesn't the sentence appear to us as something isolated and dead, if we, for example, think carefully about its essence, meaning, its thought, etc.," one can say that we are then moving deeper within the system of language' (PG 104). Only by means of a retrospective inquiry do we discover the system in which the thought lives, and move about in it. Language is, therefore, neither process nor a state, nor something present at hand. It is just the system of an institutionalized being-able-to.

Because language is an institutionalized being-able-to, one can express every meaning, say something novel in the pre-existing system. That language, however, is not objectively present as a system in speaking is shown by our being able to express meaning without knowing how we produce the individual sounds. 'Man possesses the ability to construct languages capable of expressing every sense, without having any idea how the individual sounds are produced' (T 4.002).

III

93 The power of speaking a language is a system towards which all elements of language itself point.

94 A language is a system and a sentence is a sentence of a language. That means that I call all the members of a language 'sentences'. Therefore, there also are no isolated sentences (see PG 122, 124).

95 I can be inwardly conscious of a system in 'a lightning-like thought' which I then unfold by uttering it (see PI 320).

96 Because every part implicitly refers to the whole and because therefore what is said is supported by what is unsaid, the simplest thing said becomes also enormously complicated if we should want to determine it in speech. That means that there are enormously complicated, but silent, agreements that enter into the understanding of language.

If I wanted to say a sentence such as 'this chair is brown' in such a way that no objections against the ambiguity deriving from it could be made, it would become endlessly long (see NB, p. 5). 'It is therefore also clear to the *unprejudiced mind* that the meaning of the sentence "the watch lies on the table" is more complicated than the sentence itself.

'The conventions of our language are extraordinarily complicated. There is an enormous amount of things added in thought to every proposition which are not said' (NB, p. 70). If there are enormously complicated, but silent, conventions and an enormous amount of things left unsaid in language, the apparent vagueness of normal propositions is also accounted for.

Every proposition which has a meaning says what it says. But it must not, as this proposition, also say in addition what it does not say, but could (see NB, p. 61).

IV

97 Language is language activity, institutionalized being-able-to. In language we make ourselves understood. We motivate one another reciprocally, we engage in action. And there is no such thing as action alone. There is only action in common. That is: language is the communal life-praxis of men. 'Without language we cannot influence other people in such-and-such

ways; cannot build roads and machines, etc. And also: without the use of speech and writing people could not communicate' (PI 491). Can one say: without language we could not communicate with one another? That sounds as if there could be understanding without language. The concept of language, however, resides in the concept of understanding itself, that is, in the concept of a communal form of life (see PG 140).

The essence of linguistic communication is not the transmission of information but coming to understanding within the matrix of communal action (see PI 363).

V

98 Because language is an institutionalized being-able-to, because it is from the beginning the element of a communal form of life, there is no private language.

A private language presupposes a common and public language. What is private language supposed to look like? Three traits characterize it: its words are related to what only the speaker knows; they are related to the private sensations of the speaker; whence it follows that another person cannot understand this language. 'A human being can encourage himself, give himself orders, obey, blame and punish himself; he can ask himself a question and answer it. We could even imagine human beings who spoke only in monologue; who accompanied their activities by talking to themselves. – An explorer who watched them and listened to their talk might succeed in translating their language into ours. (. . .)

'But could we also imagine a language in which a person could write down or give vocal expression to his inner experiences – his feelings, moods, and the rest – for his private use? – Well, can't we do so in our ordinary language? – But that is not what I mean. The individual words of this language are to refer to what can only be known to the person speaking; to his immediate private sensations. So another person cannot understand this language' (PI 243).

99 But now how are words *related* to sensations? Does the child set up, say, an association, a connection, between the pain

and, for example, the name which we furnish to the child if it has a pain? I can only give a name, or call something by name, however, if I already have a language at my disposal. If the form of life that is pain behaviour did not already exist, then we could not furnish to a child the use of the word 'toothache'.

'Well let us assume the child is a genius and itself invents a name for the sensation! – But then, of course, he could not make himself understood when he used the word. – So does he understand the name, without being able to explain its meaning to anyone? – But what does it mean to say that he has "named his pain"? – How has he done this naming of pain?! And whatever he did, what was its purpose? – When one says "He gave a name to his sensation" one forgets that a great deal of stage-setting in the language is presupposed if the mere act of naming is to make sense. And when we speak of someone's having given a name to pain, what is presupposed is the existence of the grammar of the word "pain"; it shows the post where the new word is stationed' (PI 257; see NFL, p. 290).

100   Let us just assume that I had connected a definite sensation with the sign S. How do I know that also in the future I will remember correctly the connection set up by me? 'One would like to say here: what will always appear to me as correct is correct. And that only means that here one cannot be speaking of "correct"' (PI 258).

I at one time connected a sensation with the sign S. If then another time I compare something with S, how then do I really know what I mean by S? A description has to be independent of that with which it is compared if I want to test it in regard to its correctness. S would therefore have to be independent of the sensation with which I have connected it. But that it is not and, therefore, one cannot speak of 'correct'. I can only mean something by S in a language in which S already means something.

If I connect a sensation with a sign as I have just described, then I cannot give a definition of it. I cannot even point to the sensation. For even an indicative definition presupposes language as already given. But could I give to myself a private verbal explanation, undertake inwardly to use the word in such a way? I can indeed undertake to apply a word in such and such a way because I already know what it means to apply a word and already am in command of this technique (see PI 262).

The ground for giving something a name in any way whatever is in need of a justification, and that in a common language. Even if we should want to reduce the giving of a name to the barest minimum or even only let out a scream, the minimal naming activity would already belong to the common language, and what the cry is supposed to mean would have to be described in the common language. 'What reason have we for calling "S" the sign for a *sensation*? For "sensation" is a word of our common language, not of one intelligible to me alone. So the use of the word stands in need of a justification which everybody understands. – And it would not help either to say that it need not be a *sensation*; that when he writes "S", he has *something* – and that is all that can be said. "Has" and "something" also belong to our common language. – So in the end when one is doing philosophy one gets to the point where one would like just to emit an inarticulate sound. – But such a sound is an expression as it occurs in a particular language-game, which should now be described' (PI 261).

101   There are no private sensations. If I can grasp and express a sensation it is no longer private. Accordingly it is nonsensical to proceed on the understanding that our private sensations – therefore, only what each person alone would now have, understand for himself – made the use of our words meaningful. Since the private is supposed to be that about which another can know nothing, the idea of a private exemplar of a sensation, to which we could inwardly and privately point in order to express our sensations, is redundant and irrelevant.

What matters is to show on what foundation we speak and make ourselves understood to one another. Everything which goes beyond that is wheels which move nothing; we can shorten our explanations about this useless and false matter.

'The essential thing about private experience is really not that each person possesses his own exemplar, but that nobody knows whether other people also have *this* or something else. The assumption would thus be possible – though unverifiable – that one section of mankind has one sensation of red and another section another' (PI 272).

Let us imagine a man who always describes with the same word different exemplars of sensations, but who would still use this word in the way we all do in the language-games to which this word belongs. In that case one can only say: if one can turn a wheel without anything else turning too, then this wheel does not belong to the machine (see PI 271).

'If I say of myself that it is only from my own case that I know what the word "pain" means – must I not say the same of other people too? And how can I generalize the *one* case so irresponsibly?

'Now someone tells me that *he* knows what pain is only from his own case! – Suppose everyone had a box with something in it: we call it a "beetle". No one can look into anyone else's box, and everyone knows what a beetle is only by looking at *his* beetle. – Here it would be quite possible for everyone to have something different in his box. One might even imagine such a thing constantly changing. – But suppose the word "beetle" had a use in these people's language? – If so it would not be used as the name of a thing. The thing in the box has no place in the language-game at all; not even as *something*: for the box might even be empty. – No. One can "divide through" by the thing in the box; it cancels out, whatever it is' (PI 293).

VI

102 The problem of a private language is closely related to the problem of solipsism. If I say, for example: 'I do not know what he is seeing when he says that he is seeing a red patch', then the difficulty arises only for the very reason that with the words 'what he is seeing' I mean a sensation in his head. Obviously I cannot stick my head into his and accordingly cannot see what is 'found' in his head. But that is also completely unimportant. For it is not a matter of our both seeing the objects which are found in our heads but rather those which are in front of our heads. We solve the puzzle by (perhaps still) saying: 'I don't know what he is seeing but I do know what he is looking at. And that is the same thing that I also am looking at' (BB, p. 61).

103   On the contrary I could also say: 'Only what I "see" is really seen.' In this case it is essential that the other is not capable of seeing what I see. I can also take that even further and exclude the other person's being able to understand at all what I mean. But if what I am saying has any meaning at all then it also has this meaning for me only through the common use, which, however, characterizes the meaning.

We may not here erroneously confuse our case with the case in which the other person does not understand what I say because he does not have sufficient information.

Of course I could say – but that is something quite different – that my position here is an exception, that the sentence: 'Only I really see' means that I am precisely the one who gives the meaning and that this is not characterized through the common use. 'And therefore, if I utter the sentence "Only I really see", it is conceivable that my fellow creatures thereupon will arrange their notation so as to fall in with me by saying "so-and-so is really seen" instead of "L.W. sees so-and-so", etc., etc. What, however, is wrong, is to think that I can *justify* this choice of notation' (BB, p. 66).

VII

104   But now what is this thing called language about which we are always speaking here? Language – what we are calling language – is the language of our everyday life.

'When I talk about language (words, sentences, etc.) I must speak the language of everyday. Is this language somehow too coarse and material for what we want to say? *Then how is another one to be constructed?* – And how strange that we should be able to do anything at all with the one we have!

'In giving explanations I already have to use language full-blown (not some sort of preparatory, provisional one); this by itself shows that I can adduce only exterior facts about language.

'Yes, but then how can these explanations satisfy us? – Well, your very questions were framed in this language; they had to be expressed in this language, if there was anything to ask' (PI 120)!

Since we are always inside language and remain inside it, what we say about language is something 'external' in so far as it does not touch it, does not alter it from the inside. It is nothing other than just – language.

Above all else, therefore, the apparatus of our customary language is what we call language. We call other apparatuses language, then, by analogy or in comparison with it (see PI 494).

In considering language one could easily come to the point of thinking that in philosophy one is not speaking about words and sentences in a completely homely sense, but in a sublime, abstract sense. But in philosophy we are not able to attain to a greater universality than in what we say in life. What I say about language I have to say in the language of everyday. In philosophy I have to already use the full language. It is not first in philosophy that I come to language, but I am already in it. In a certain way, therefore, in philosophy I can only express something external about language. That is, I cannot speak about language as if I stood outside of language. It is only in and with language that I can speak about language. In this way I can discover something new. In this way I can ask questions and find satisfying answers (see PG 77).

105 Logic could appear to us as a sort of normative language of language, as the norm of an ideal language, to which we, in our everyday language, only approximate. This would be a misunderstanding. For logic does not exist in a vacuum, but it shows how everyday language functions. Naturally we are able to construct ideal languages for definite ends, but they are then not ideals. Rather they are poorer and narrower than the language of everyday and need it in order to be construed and interpreted.

'F. P. Ramsey once emphasized in conversation with me that logic was a "normative science". I do not know exactly what he had in mind, but it was doubtless closely related to what only dawned on me later; namely, that in philosophy we often *compare* the use of words with games and calculi which have fixed rules, but cannot say that someone who is using language *must* be playing such a game. – But if you say that our language only *approximates* to such calculi you are standing on the very brink of a misunderstanding. For then it may look as if what we were talking about were an *ideal* language. As if our logic were, so to speak, a logic for a vacuum. – Whereas logic does not treat of language – or of thought – in the sense in which a natural science treats of a natural phenomenon, and the most that can be said is that we *construct* ideal languages. But the word "ideal" is liable to mislead, for it sounds as if these languages were better, more perfect, than our everyday language; and as if it took the logician to show people at last what a proper sentence looked like' (PI 81).

106 Language is the only language there is. The language in which I speak about language is language itself.

'I formerly believed that there exists an everyday language in which we all normally speak and a primary language which expresses what we really know, that is, the phenomena. I also spoke about a first and a second system. (. . .) I now believe that we essentially have only one language, and that is ordinary language' (W, p. 45).

107 We can, however, in everyday language extend partial systems of everyday language. As, for example, when we distinguish the language of visual space and the language of Euclidean space. Visual space has, that is, a non-Euclidean structure. From mixing up such languages, as for example these two, there arise great confusions (see W, p. 59).

108 Because objects play so great a role for us and because this characterizes everyday language, it is difficult for us to describe genuine phenomena in everyday language (see W, p. 258). All too often we look for things, for objects, where there are simply no things at all.

G

UNDERSTANDING

I

109 Language can only function through understanding, intending, interpreting, and thinking (see BB, pp. 3). The concept of a language lies in the concept of an agreement. Understanding and an agreement belong together.

110 Agreement presupposes that the other person uses and understands the language the way I do (see PR 7). He does not, therefore, need to understand the individual words. If in certain situations we again and again hear someone expressing an experience in a foreign language, then we can understand this without understanding the words individually.

'Someone who cannot speak English hears me on certain occasions cry out: "What lovely light!" He guesses the meaning and now uses the expression himself as I do, but without understanding the three words. Does he understand the expression?' (z 150.) It is also possible analogously to invent cases in which one does not express an experience and to ask oneself what it means to guess the meaning (see z 151, 152). When a reader, for example, reads in a story the sentence: 'He sized him up with hostile glances and said. . .', he understands this and at first does not doubt it. He could then doubt it and ask himself whether the hostile sizing up was feigned. He then guesses the meaning from the context (see PI 652).

'Just in this way we refer by the phrase "understanding a word" not necessarily to that which happens while we are saying or hearing it, but to the whole environment of the event of saying it' (BB, p. 157).

111   Understanding is no special process which accompanies the perception of a sentence. 'I understand the sentence by using it. Understanding is, therefore, not at all a special process, but it is operating with the sentence. *The sentence is there for the purpose of our operating with it*' (w, p. 167).

112   Understanding is therefore neither a process nor a state.

A process has duration, and so does a state. An example of a conscious process is when I recite a poem to myself in my head. That is a process which has a beginning, a middle and an end. I can even measure its duration. It is a consious process because no one perceives it in distinction from the reciting of a poem out loud.

If I say: 'What lovely light' and understand it, then understanding it is no process which accompanies this intelligent uttering in the way that when climbing a stairs I can silently count the steps.

If someone should say to us that an activity which he knows well and which he performs were accompanied by an inner state, then we would answer him: 'That does not interest us. We indeed see that you know your way about it well.'

'How would we counter someone who told us that with *him* understanding was an inner process? – How should we counter him if he said that with him knowing how to play chess was an inner process? – We should say that when we want to know if he can play chess we aren't interested in anything that goes on inside him. – And if he replies that this is in fact just what we are interested in, that is, we are interested in whether he can play chess – then we shall have to draw his attention to the criteria which would demonstrate his capacity, and on the other hand to the criteria for all "inner states"' (pi, p. 181). However, we also do not call understanding the activity which shows us comprehension, but that which the activity points to, that which the activity is an index for: therefore, a power, and a constant one, at that.

Knowing, understanding, being able to, capacity, one will want to call a state (see pg 104). I can describe the course or the state of my pains; can I also describe the course of my understanding? How do I observe my understanding, my being able to? A psychic state has a duration. I can say: 'I hoped all day

long.' But I cannot say: 'I understood all day long.' In the case
of a state which endures one can describe its alterations. But
can I follow with attention the forgetting of something known
(see z 75–81)?

If one wants to call understanding a state, then one could
only do it in the sense in which one speaks of the state of a
body, of a physical model, or in which one speaks of the unconscious states of a model of the soul. If I say: 'I have
unconscious toothaches' then that is a very special way of using
the concept of 'state' (see PG 104).

We are tempted again and again to imagine psycho-physio-
logical or spiritual mechanisms as the foundations of our
abiilties. '. . . we are strongly inclined to use the metaphor of
something being in a peculiar state for saying that something
can behave in a particular way. And this way of representation,
or this metaphor, is embodied in the expressions "He is capable
of . . .", "He is able to multiply large numbers in his head" "He
can play chess": in these sentences the verb is used in the
present tense, suggesting that the phrases are descriptions of
states which exist at the moment we speak.

'The same tendency shows itself in our calling the ability to
solve a mathematical problem, the ability to enjoy a piece of
music, etc., certain states of the mind; we don't mean by this
expression "conscious mental phenomena". Rather, a state of
the mind in this sense is the state of a hypothetical mechanism,
a mind model meant to explain the conscious mental phenomena. (Such things as unconscious or subconscious mental
states are features of the mind *model*.) In this way also we can
hardly help conceiving of memory as of a kind of storehouse.
Note also how sure people are that to the ability to add or to
multiply or to say a poem by heart, etc., there *must* correspond
a peculiar state of the person's brain, although on the other
hand they know next to nothing about such psycho-physio-
logical correspondences. We regard these phenomena as mani-
festations of this mechanism, and their possibility is the particular construction of the mechanism itself' (BB, p. 117–18). Even
if these uncritically imagined mechanisms existed, they could
not explain understanding to us. If understanding is not a
process and not a state, then it can also not be the consequence
of a state conceived of as usual.

II

113   A power (*Können*) is a possible acting that is ahead of itself, namely, in everything that it can do. Understanding is oriented toward totality and is thereby already something total. We make that clear to ourselves when we ask: from what point do we understand a sentence? When it is half utttered, or completely uttered, or while we express it? The answer runs: I already understand the sentence when I begin to say it because I understand the language and already can. For: 'Something is a sentence only in a language. To understand a sentence means to understand a language' (PG 84).

A similar situation exists if I remember a melody. If I search for a melody and it suddenly occurs to me, then it stands completely before my mind without its having, however, totally occurred to me in this moment. 'I want to remember a melody and it escapes me; suddenly I say: "Now I know it!" and I sing it. What was it like to suddenly know it? Surely it can't have occurred to me *in its entirety* in that moment! – Perhaps you will say: "It's a particular feeling, as if it were *there*" – but *is* it there? Suppose I now begin to sing it and get stuck? – But may I not have been *certain* at that moment that I knew it? So in some sense or other it was *there* after all! – But in what sense? You would say that the melody was there, if, say, someone sang it through, or heard it mentally from beginning to end. I am not, of course, denying that the statement that the melody is there can also be given a quite different meaning – for example, that I have a bit of paper on which it is written. – And what does his being "certain", his knowing it, consist in? – Of course we can say: if someone says with conviction that now he knows the tune, then it is (somehow) present to his mind in its entirety at that moment – and this is a definition of the expression "the tune is present to his mind in its entirety" ' (PI 184). If I intend to whistle you a melody, have I then, say, already whistled it in my thoughts (see z 2)?

'Standing before the mind in its entirety' is the mode of givenness of a power.

114   Of course I already understand a sentence when I begin to say it, but not all at once, as it were in advance, in a non-discursive intuition. Rather, understanding unfolds itself, explicates itself, in speaking.

115   We are inclined to call understanding two things: knowing that I can do something and the exercise of the power, doing itself (see PG 11). In the case of following an order we find: (1) knowing that I have to do something and what it is that I have to do and at the same time knowing that I can do it and (2) the leap towards doing. In following an order understanding as a power is shown especially clearly (see PG 8). Knowing and being-able-to belong together. ' "To understand a word" can mean: *to know* how it is used. *Being able to* use it' (PG 10).

116   But if that means knowing the grammatical possibility of its use, then I can ask: do I have to have the whole way of using it in my head? I have it in my head. But how? Just as, for example, the chess player has in his head the rules of chess but also, at the same time, the ABC and the multiplication table. Knowing is, so to speak, a reservoir and this reservoir is a constant, latent being-able-to (see PG 10). I always, that is, 'know' and not just when I am thinking about it or applying my knowledge (see PI 148). But in no case are we dealing here with an unconscious state. That constant, latent being-able-to has nothing to do with 'unconsciousness' nor, as we saw, with a state (see PI 149). 'The grammar of the word "knows" is evidently closely related to that of "can", "is able to". But also closely related to that of "understands". ("Mastery of a technique.")' (PI 150).

117   In that I understand something, know something, am able to do something, master something, I can do it in its entirety. Here is shown the unfolding totality of understanding. Because, however, understanding is a whole, so to say, a constant background, I do not need to unfold it as a whole in order to become conscious of it. This shows the application of the expression: now I know it! Now I understand! Now I can do it! I say this, for example, when I grasp the law of a series. But I have no need then to continue the series to infinity (see PI 151). No limit

can be given to how long I have to continue the series. Understanding means, namely, that one continues the series up to this or that number: that is only an application of understanding. Understanding itself is that out of which the use arises. Still in that case the application remains precisely a criterion of understanding (see PI 146). Understanding is not something hidden or something which stands for something else which I still have to look for. I understand because I understand and this 'because' is: to know and to be able to.

III

118   Understanding is just as much a lightning-like event which puts together a number of items and makes us understand it as it is also an unfolding explication (see PI 319, 320).

If I understand a game then, on the one hand, I understand it in its entirety and beforehand and, on the other hand, my understanding first shows itself in playing itself.

'Just as, if one should ask: at what point can you play chess? Always? Or while you say that you can do it? Or during a move? And how strange that being-able-to play chess takes so short a time and a game of chess so much longer! (Augustine: '*when* do I measure a period of time?')

'It can seem to us as if the grammatical rules were in some sense the explication of what we, in the use of a word, experience all at once' (PG 12). It may appear here that the act of signifying includes grammar, that grammar would be contained in it, like a string of pearls in a box out of which we would only have to extract them. This picture misleads us. Understanding is not an instantaneous grasping of something, out of which later only the consequences have to be derived, but it is at one and the same time precisely instantaneous and unfolding (see PG 18; RFM 1–130).

119   While we seem on the one hand to possess understanding lightning-like, on the other hand we never possess it in its entirety. The totality of understanding is not a totality of possession. 'It disturbs us, as it were, that the thought of a sentence is not present in its entirety in a moment. We consider

it as an object which we produce and never totally possess, for no sooner does one part arise than another part disappears' (z 153).

IV

120   The totality of understanding is a system.

A system is in some way an infinity because I can investigate it endlessly. A system is an infinity, but one such that it can be grasped all at once. We will get clearer about the problem of finiteness and infinity if we consider the understanding of a distance, of a series, and that of space and time.

121   Can we at all grasp an infinite stretch? What can that mean?

Someone says: 'I can imagine an infinitely high telegraph pole.' 'Good. And how do you verify that? How do you verify, for example, that a telegraph pole is 10 metres high?' 'By putting a measuring stick up against it.' 'Do you want, therefore, to put an infinite measuring stick up against the infinitely high pole? And what is the criterion that it is infinite?' (see w, pp. 187f).

We cannot think an infinite stretch as verified by means of an endless pacing off, for, if the pacing off is endless, then it does not lead to its goal. If the path of the pacing or the measuring is endless, it does not bring me to the point of seeing over the whole stretch (see PG, pp. 455ff). If we knew infinity only from its description, then this description would exist, and nothing else. We would be endlessly busied with describing the infinite (see PR 135).

I can understand an infinite stretch. Then I already see that infinite is not the same as endless. For I cannot verify by an endless series of steps the proposition about the infinite stretch. I can do so only by *one* step (see PR 123).

To grasp *all* the numbers successively is impossible, and is without meaning. Certainly, a successive grasping of numbers is possible, but that naturally does not lead to a totality. Totality is only present as a concept (see PR 124).

122   What we call infinite is nothing other than a possibility.

The infinite series of numbers is only the infinite possibility of finite series of numbers. In the signs themselves is found only the possibility and not the reality of repetition (see PR 144).

'Our normal way of speaking bears the seeds of confusion right into its foundations, by using, on the one hand, the word "series" in the sense of "extension" and on the other hand in the sense of "law". One can get clear about the relation of the two by considering a machine which makes coil springs. In this case a wire is shoved through a passage wound *in the form of a helix*. This passage produces as many windings of the coil as one wants. What one calls the infinite helix is not perhaps something like endless pieces of wire or something that these approximate to the longer they become, but the law of the helix as it is embodied in the short passage. The expression "infinite helix" or "infinite series" is, therefore, misleading' (PG, p. 430).

Nevertheless, the infinite possibility of repetition, that is, of use, is not proven. For it is only a possibility and not a necessity. 'We ought not to mistake the infinite possibility of its application for what has really been proved. The infinite possibility of application has *not* been proved!' (PR 163.)

'The infinite appears in language always in the same way, namely, as a closer determination of the concept *possible*. (. . .) Infinite possibility does not mean: possibility of the infinite. The word "infinite" characterizes a possibility and not a reality' (W, p. 228f).

'If we would like to say that infinity is a property of possibility, not of reality, or: the word "infinite" always belongs to the word "possible" and such like, – that amounts to saying: the word "infinite" is always a part of a *rule*' (PR, p. 313).

123   Now we also understand why the reasoning that leads to an endless regress has to be abandoned. Not because we could not reach the goal in that way, because there is no road to infinity, not even an endless one, but rather because here there simply is no goal. Endlessness itself shows that the lack of a goal is to be gathered from the starting point itself (see Z 693).

124   What makes us believe that there are perhaps infinitely many things is mistaking the things of physics for elements of

knowledge. Only the *possible* combinations of things are infinite
(see PR 147).

125　If I always see only a finite number of things, where then
do I get my knowledge of the infinite? The infinite is not a
number or a quantity. The infinite is already given to me –
intentionally – in the experience of the finite. Precisely because
I experience the finite as finite, I see the possibility of
further finite experiences. And this possibility has no determined
end.

　'But if I always see only a finite number of things, divisions,
colours, etc., then there is just no infinity at all; in no sense.
The feeling here is:

　'If I always see only so few things, then there is nothing more
at all. As if the case were the following: if I see only 4, then
there are just not 100. But infinity does not have the status
of a number. It is quite correct: if I see only 4 there are
not 100 and also not 5. But an infinite possibility does exist
which is satisfied just as little by a small number as a large
one. The reason for this, in fact, is because it itself is *not* a
quantity.

　'We all know, of course, what it means to say that there is an
infinite possibility and a finite reality, for we say that time and
physical space are infinite, but we could always see or experience only finite parts of them. But where do I get the knowledge
about something infinite at all? I must, therefore, in some senses
have two kinds of experiences: one of the finite, which it cannot
surpass (this idea of surpassing is in itself senseless), and one
of the infinite. And that is also the way it is. Experience as a
living experience of facts gives me the finite; the objects *contain*
the infinite. Of course, not as a quantity competing with the
finite experience, but in the intentional order. Not as if I saw a
space that is practically empty and with only a completely
small, finite experience in it. But rather in space I see the
possibility of every finite experience. That is, no experience can
be too large for it or exhaust it. That is not perhaps because we
are familiar with the dimensions of every experience and know
space to be larger, but we understand that that belongs to the
essence of space. – We recognize this infinite essence of space in
the smallest part.

'What is already senseless is that one so often thinks that a large number would be indeed closer to the infinite than a small number.

'As said, the infinite does not compete with the finite. It is what essentially excludes nothing finite' (PR 138).

The problem of the 'infinite divisibility' makes this especially clear to us. If we say: space is infinitely – or unlimitedly – divisible, then this means that space is not made up of individual parts, but that it offers us the possibility of dividing it as often as one wants.

'How is it with the case of infinite divisibility? Let us consider that it makes sense to say that every finite number of parts is thinkable but no infinite number; but that just in that consists infinite divisibility. "Any" does not now mean that the *totality of all* divisions is thinkable (which it is not, for it does not exist). But the *variable* "divisibility" (that is, the concept of divisibility) exists which *sets no limits* around actual divisibility; and its infinity consists in that. . . .

'As if infinite possibility were the possibility of an infinite number.

'And that again shows that we are dealing with two different meanings of the word "possible" if I say: "the line can be divided into three parts" and on the other hand say: "the line is infinitely divisible". (. . .)

'What does it mean that a patch in visual space can be divided into three parts? It can only mean that a proposition which describes a patch divided in that way has a meaning. (If it is not a matter of confusing the divisibility of physical objects with that of a patch in visual space.)

'On the contrary, infinite – or better *unlimited* – divisibility does not mean that there is a proposition which describes a line divided into infinitely many parts, for there is no such proposition. This possibility is, therefore, not indicated by any reality of signs, but by a possibility of another kind of signs themselves.

'If one says: space is infinitely divisible, that really means: space is not made up of individual things (parts).

'Infinite divisibility means in a certain sense that space is indivisible, that dividing it up does not touch *it*. That it has nothing to do with it: *it* does not consist of parts. It says, as it were, to reality: you can do in me what you want. (You can be divided up in me as often as you want.) Space gives reality an infinite opportunity of being divided' (PR 139).

126   It is not possible to inquire to infinity (see w, p. 114). The 'really infinite' is a 'mere word' (see z 274). If I am supposed to imagine an infinitely long row of balls or an infinitely long stick, I observe that I cannot do it (see z 275).

    But can I not then imagine that a row of trees runs on without end (see z 272)? But is that the same thing as imagining an infinite row? 'The concept "and so forth" symbolized by '. . .' – is one of the most important of all and (. . .) infinitely fundamental' (NB, p. 89).

127   We do not apprehend time as an infinite reality but we apprehend it *intentionally* as an infinite reality. That means that, on the one hand, we cannot think of an infinite period of time and, on the other hand, cannot imagine that some day is the last, that time, therefore, has an end. This having-no-end belongs to the nature of time. The filled time that we are familiar with is limited, finite. Infinity is an inner quality of the form of time (see PR 143). Time has *now* the possibility of all the future in it (see PR 140). 'Infinity lies in the nature of time, it is not its accidental elongation' (PR 143). So life without end is thinkable rather as spatial series without end because we cannot sense life as closed. Rather an infinite spatial series would have to be already present as a whole.

128   What is infinite in endlessness is finiteness.

V

129   We have now to get clear about the fact that – as will also be shown still more clearly in the course of our further inquiries – we do not call understanding *one* phenomenon, but rather a set of phenomena which are more or less related to one another. These phenomena are shown in their multiplicity in the actual use of the language or languages that we have learned (see PG 35). I can become aware of this multiplicity if a number of words are read aloud to me and I am supposed to say 'yes' or

'no' to them according to whether I understand them or not. Accordingly I try to remember what happened each time I understood. Then I discover that it is something manifold. This manifold understanding is sometimes characterized by its circumstances, and it is gradual. This is similar to what happens in the case of voluntary and involuntary action. Namely it is also at times characterized by a multiplicity of circumstances and it can, at any given time, be more or less voluntary (or involuntary) (see BB, p. 157).

130 The unity-constituting affinity belonging to the common element in the process cannot, however, be defined by a generic term.

The category leads us, that is, to look for something identical possessed in common by all the events, whereas in reality there are only things standing in relation.

'One says: If I use the word "understand" in all these cases, then there also has to be something identical in them, which is precisely what is essential to understanding (expecting, wishing, etc.). For why otherwise would I be supposed to call them by the same name?

'This argument proceeds from the notion that it is what is common to the processes, or objects, etc., which has to justify their being characterized by a common category.

'This notion is, in a certain sense, *too primitive*. What the generic term indicates is, however, a relationship between objects, but this relationship must not be the common possession of a property or of a constituent part. It can bind the members together in chainlike fashion, so that one is related to another *by means of intermediate members;* and two members which are close to one another can have characteristics in common, be *similar* to one another, while those members which are more distant have nothing more in common with one another and still belong to the same family. Indeed, even if a characteristic is common to all the members of the family, it does not have to be the one which defines the concept.

'The relationship of the members falling under the concept ran be the result of the sharing in common of characteristics whose appearance in the family of the concept overlaps in the most highly complicated fashion' (PG 35).

The living relationship which resides in the manifold processes of understanding would be levelled by a common concept. Such a relationship cannot be brought under one concept (*sich einholen*).

Here we stand before a very important, more general, phenomenon that concerns not only understanding.

The usual general concept appears to contain the specific experience of what is common to all the compared events. But there is no such specific experience. For if it is an experience then it stands beside the mass of other experiences whose specific common element it is indeed supposed to be. With that it has lost its purpose, for it was supposed to do as an individual what now precisely the mass of compared experiences accomplishes (see BB, p. 86).

Therefore, we have to replace the normal universal concept not by a new concept but by a new system of concepts (*Begrifflichkeit*): a family resemblance. 'And the result of this examination is: we see a complicated network of similarities overlapping and criss-crossing: sometimes overall similarities, sometimes similarities of detail.

'I can think of no better expression to characterize these similarities than "family resemblances"; the various resemblances between members of a family: build, features, colour of eyes, gait, temperament, etc., etc. overlap and criss-cross in the same way –' (PI 66, 67).

By category or generic concept, then, we should understand not the normal universal concept but a family resemblance. We should, however, not only be on our guard before the normal general concepts because they level understanding and do not bring it into a unity (*einholen*), but also because they threaten to undercut and to overlook what is specific and concrete, without which the universal simply is not. Thus it can happen that one does not discover precisely that very concrete item which would contribute the most to the understanding of the general characterization which one is considering.

'The idea that in order to get clear about the meaning of a general term one had to find the common element in all its applications has shackled philosophical investigation; for it has not only led to no result, but also made the philosopher dismiss as irrelevant the concrete cases, which alone could have helped him to understand the usage of the general term' (BB, pp. 19–20).

VI

131 We can learn to understand, for we can learn language, and understanding is deposited in language. By learning a language I understand language. 'Learning a language *effects* its understanding' (PG 3).

That is, I learn language, or understanding, or thought, under certain circumstances. I do not thereby learn to describe these circumstances but just: to understand (see Z 114). Understanding detaches itself from the circumstances. 'The way we learn language is not *contained* in our use of it' (PG 39).

The way I came to understanding can, to be sure, be something external and accidental which has nothing more to do with understanding itself. 'In what I understand the way I have come to it disappears. Then I understand what I understand. That is, the accidental circumstance can only be related to something external, as, say, if one says: "I discovered that after I drank strong coffee." The coffee is no longer contained in what I discovered' (PR 157).

132 But the way understanding makes its appearance is as something sudden and unforeseen. For this reason one person cannot order another: understand that! And when understanding has suddenly made its appearance, it is there and, from its side, cannot be further explained (see Z 158). When a person suddenly understands, nothing happens other than that he understands (see PI 321, 322).

133 Understanding is: 'because' I know it. I cannot explain any further this 'because'; at most, for the sake of explanation, I can point to something comparable.

'Understanding a sentence is much more akin to understanding a theme in music than one may think. What I mean is that understanding a sentence lies nearer than one thinks to what is ordinarily called understanding a musical theme. Why is just *this* the pattern of variation in loudness and tempo? One would

like to say: "Because I know what it's all about." But what is
it all about? I should not be able to say. In order to "explain"
I could only compare it with something else which has the
same rhythm (I mean the same pattern). (One says: "Don't you
see, this is as if a conclusion were being drawn" or: "This is as
it were a parenthesis", etc. How does one justify such com-
parisons? – There are very different kinds of justification here)'
(PI 527).

I can translate the explanation of the musical picture into the
picture of another event. Then the two pictures mutually
illuminate and explain one another (see PG 4; PI, p. 178).

'We speak of understanding a sentence in the sense in which
it can be replaced by another which says the same; but also in
the sense in which it cannot be replaced by any other. (Any
more than one musical theme can be replaced by another.)

'In the one case the thought in the sentence is something
common to different sentences; in the other, something that is
expressed only by these words in these positions. (Understanding
a poem)' (PI 531).

134   If I understand a sentence or, for example, a picture, then
I say: I understand it *in this way*. This 'in this way' can have
two meanings. It can mean a transitive, translating understanding in which I translate the understanding into something else.
That is, in understanding one thing I think about another
(see PG 37). This is similar to when we also 'explain the understanding of a gesture as a translation into words, and the understanding of words as a translation into gestures.

'And we actually will explain words by a gesture and a
gesture by words' (PG 5). I transfer precisely out of one symbolism into another. 'We also say: "I understand this picture
exactly. I could model it in clay"' (PG 7).

The expression 'in this way' (*so*) can, however, also mean an
intransitive understanding. In that case, I do not think about
something else, and what is understood is quasi-autonomous,
like the understanding of a melody (see PG 37).

VII

135   In all cases, however, all translating, interpreting, deciphering comes to an ultimate understanding, to something final. An interpretation leaves several possibilities open. It is *this* interpretation in contrast to another. If we were to say: every sentence needs another interpretation, another act of construing, that would mean that no sentence (*Satz*) can be understood without a supplement (*Zusatz*). But if someone asks me what time it is then I do not interpret. And if someone takes up a knife and comes after me, then I do not say: I interpret that as a threat (see PG 9). Rather I stand here before something immediate and final. If one has come to something ultimate then it is not possible to question any longer.

‘ “He said these words, but did not think about what he was saying.” – “That is not right, I did think about something.” – “And *what* then?” – “Well, what I said.” To the statement “this sentence makes sense” one cannot really ask: “which” Just as to the sentence “this combination of words is a sentence” one cannot ask: “which?” ’ (PG 13).

136   We are inclined to look behind understanding for another, more distant, understanding that grounds it. If I understand something and express it, then I understand. Then the expression expresses my understanding. There is no second understanding which would remain unexpressed. It can be that I express a pseudo-understanding; but then we are simply not dealing with understanding. It can also be that I have and recognize a first, illuminating understanding, that I could penetrate more deeply into the understanding of what I understand. But then this first understanding is also a complete understanding, for it understands itself as initial. And this understanding is completely expressed. If the understanding which is supposed to underlie understanding is not expressed by this, because it would be essentially inexpressible, then it simply makes no sense to inquire after a more complete expression of an understanding represented in this way.

‘A sentence is given me in unfamiliar code together with the key for deciphering it. Then, in a certain sense, everything required for the understanding of the sentence has been given me. And yet if I were asked whether I understood the sentence I should reply: "I must first decode it" and only when I had it in front of me decoded as an English sentence, would I say: "now I understand it."

'If we now raise the question: "At what moment of translating into English does understanding begin?" we get a glimpse into the nature of what we call "understanding."

' "To understand a sentence" can mean: "to know what the sentence signifies"; i.e. to be able to answer the question: "what does the sentence say?"

'It is a prevalent notion that we can only imperfectly *exhibit* our understanding; that we can only point to it from afar or come close to it, but never lay our hands on it, and that the ultimate thing can never be said. We say: "Understanding is something *different* from the expression of understanding. *Understanding* cannot be exhibited; it is something inward and spiritual." – Or: "Whatever I do to exhibit understanding, whether I repeat an explanation of a word, or carry out an order to show that I have understood it, these bits of behaviour do not *have* to be taken as proofs of understanding." Similarly, people also say: "I cannot show anyone else my toothache; I cannot *prove* to anyone else that I have toothache." But the impossibility spoken of here is supposed to be a logical one. "Isn't it the case that the expression of understanding is always an incomplete expression?" That means, I suppose, an expression with something missing – but the something missing is essentially *inexpressible*, because otherwise I might find a better expression for it. And "essentially inexpressible" means that it makes no sense to talk of a more complete expression' (PG 6).

137   An ultimate understanding is the criterion for testing and for justification (see PI 265).

VIII

138   What leads us to want to still proceed beyond something ultimate is the mixing up of cause and ground or reason. One is

lured into this confusion by the equivocal use of the word 'why'. This ambivalence can be discovered especially easily if one considers the confusing of cause and motive in human actions. 'Thus when the chain of reasons has come to an end and still the question "why" is asked, one is inclined to give a cause instead of a reason. If, e.g., to the question: "why did you paint just this colour when I told you to paint a red patch?" you give the answer: "I have been shown a sample of this colour and the word 'red' was pronounced to me at the same time; and therefore this colour now always comes to my mind when I hear the word "red" ', then you have given a cause for your action and not a reason.

'The proposition that your action has such and such a cause is an hypothesis. The hypothesis is well-founded if one has had a number of experiences which, roughly speaking, agree in showing that your action is the regular sequel of certain conditions which we then call causes of the action. In order to know the reason which you had for making a certain statement, for acting in a particular way, etc., no number of agreeing experiences is necessary, and the statement of your reason is not an hypothesis. The differences between the grammars of "reason" and "cause" is quite similar to that between the grammars of "motive" and "cause". Of the cause one can say that one can't *know* it but only *conjecture* it. On the other hand one often says: "Surely *I* must know why I did it" talking of the *motive*. When I say: "we can only *conjecture* the cause but we *know* the motive" this statement will be seen later on to be a grammatical one. The "can" refers to *a logical* possibility.

'The double use of the word "why", asking for the cause and asking for the motive, together with the idea that we can know, and not only conjecture, our motives, gives rise to the confusion that a motive is a cause of which we are immediately aware, a cause "seen from the inside", or a cause experienced – (BB, p. 15).

139 The confusing of reason for cause concerns not only my action, in which the reason is a motive, but reality in general. Reality is then grounded if I see how it is. That is, when I have run up against final ground and therefore *the* last ground, that is, when I see it in its last-grounded sense. In that case we also

have to consider that the configuration of reality is the ground of our action.

140   When one asks about the grounds of an assumption, then one reflects upon these grounds (see PI 475). But I do not thereby conclude to causes or from causes. Rather I draw a conclusion which is not a conclusion of logic but reflection upon a sense, and which, therefore, becomes a decision (*Entschluss*). 'An inference is a transition to an assertion; and so also to the behaviour that corresponds to the assertion. "I draw the consequences" not only in words, but also in action' (PI 486). The justification of an assertion upon which I reflect is the sense of the assertion itself (see PG 40). Therein is found the ground of the assertion. And my meaningful, consequent action follows from that.

141   Our mistake is time and again to look for causes where we have long ago reached the ground where we see the proto-phenomenon. 'Our mistake is to look for an explanation where we ought to look at what happens as a "proto-phenomenon". That is, where we ought to have said: *this language-game is played*' (PI 654). One is not dealing here with an explanation of a language-game, but with the establishing of a language-game.
   We often only arrive at the correct answer when we suppress the question 'why'. Only then do we see the *facts* at all which are the answer or which lead us to the answer (see PI 471).

142   We only arrive at a final ground because the understanding of relationships is already achieved in a preliminary latent comprehension, or rather, in this latent comprehension there is found the final ground. This is shown by the fact that there is no question without a possible answer; indeed, it is shown by the fact that we only first understand the sense of a question when we consider what its answer looks like (see PR 132). And if we understand the sense of a question, we also understand the method of finding an answer to it. The sense is the method of answering, of finding out the answer (see NB, p. 44).
   I was saying: where one cannot seek there can one also not ask, and that means: where there is no logical method of finding, then the question can have no sense.

'There is a problem only where there is a method for solving it (that is not to say, of course: "there is a problem only where the solution has been found").

'That is, there is also no problem where the solution can be expected only from a sort of revelation. To a revelation there corresponds no question' (PR 149). It is often only the method of answering which shows what one is really asking about. Indeed, only the actual answering of the question shows what the question really was (see w, p. 79). Asking, seeking, finding are only possible in a system (see PR 150). There is, therefore, something which one cannot look for: the pre-given ground-system. And that is the world.

IX

143 We saw that we understand the world as a system. I can bring a world-description to a unitary form, in that I lay a 'net' over the world, for example, the Newtonian world description (see above, No. 28). That may not be confused with understanding.

144 If I have once thrown such a net over the world, then I discover laws. The laws are concerned with the net and not with what the net describes (see NB, p. 43). 'In the net-analogy of physics: although the specks are geometrical figures, geometry still is not able to say anything at all about their form and position. The net is, however, *purely* geometrical; all its properties can be given *a priori*' (NB, p. 38).

A law can neither be verified nor falsified. It is neither true nor false. It is always only probable. A statement is either true or false. What is only probable is not a statement. That a law is probable simply means that it is apt (see w, p. 100). In such a case one always bets on a possibility under the assumption of the uniformity of events covered by the net (see PR 233).

The causal law is, moreover, no law, but it is the form of a law.

'The whole modern conception of the world is founded on the illusion that the so-called laws of nature are the explanations of natural phenomena' (T 6.371).

145   We may not confuse understanding with a world description net any more than we may confuse a cause or ground with
an hypothesis. The equations of physics, for example, are not
propositions, not orders, but hypotheses. We have to make a
distinction between 'assertions' and 'hypotheses'. 'An hypothesis
is not an assertion, but a law for the construction of assertions'
(w, p. 99).

Only individual assertions can be true or false, but not an
hypothesis.

For this reason an hypothesis is also never verified. What we
can observe and therefore verify are certain individual 'cuts'
through the hypothesis, cuts through the total structure which
the hypothesis presents (see w, pp. 100, 159ff).

The hypothesis, therefore, is not susceptible to being either
verified or falsified. It is neither true nor false, but it is probable
(see w, p. 100).

The justification of an hypothesis lies in its probability. That
is, it lies in the achievement of simplification and of convenience
to which it leads.

Even if the assertions to which the hypothesis leads are false,
the hypothesis is not contradicted by this. We can put it in order
by introducing a supplementary hypothesis.

What characterizes an hypothesis are its simplicity, its
plausibility, its probability. With reference to an hypothesis
these three words are synonymous.

If we always have to form new auxiliary hypotheses in order
to sustain an hypothesis, then the hypothesis remains simple no
longer. It becomes unfit for its goal and we give it up.

The question of how many cuts I must have observed, how
many aspects I must have seen, in order to be certain of the
reality of an hypothesis, has no meaning. For nothing can prove
the hypothesis. It is neither true nor false. Its acceptance or
rejection depends exclusively on its performance.

The question of how many cuts I must have observed, how
many aspects I must have seen, in order to be certain of the
reality of an hypothesis, has no meaning. For nothing can prove
the hypothesis. It is neither true nor false. Its acceptance or
rejection depends exclusively on its performance.

The hypothesis is not a proposition whose truth is only less
certain. As if we had just not yet checked all the cases and for

this reason were less certain, as if the criterion of the truth of an hypothesis were, so to speak, an historical one. The hypothesis follows neither from a singular proposition nor from a group of singular propositions. An hypothesis is never verified (see w, pp. 210f).

But since the hypothesis generates assertions, it becomes a proposition in connection with *that* facet of such an assertion which is laid up against reality (see PG, p. 222).

We can also decide that there is to be no deviating from a certain part of an hypothesis. Then we establish a mode of representation and turn that part of the hypothesis into a *postulate*. 'A postulate has to be of such a sort that no conceivable experience can contradict it, even if it may be inconvenient in the extreme to hold on to the postulate. In the measure that one can speak here of a greater or lesser convenience, there exists a greater or lesser probability of the postulate' (PG, p. 225).

X

146 Understanding moves in the direction of an immediate ultimate. And this has to be brought out into the open. 'There must not be anything hypothetical in our considerations. We must do away with all *explanation*, and description alone must take its place' (PI 109). At one time or another one has to make the move from explanation to description (see OC 189), that is, to immediate experience.

Everything that we say has to be related in the last analysis, even if by detours, to immediate experience, if it has meaning.

What is immediately experienced is a phenomenon. It is not a symptom for something, it does not stand for something, it is itself: reality.

'All that is essential is that the signs, in no matter how complicated a fashion, be related at the end to immediate experience and not to an intermediate member (a thing in itself).

'All that is necessary for our propositions (about reality) to have a meaning is that our experience in *some* sense agree or not with them. That is, immediate experience has to prove the truth of only *something* in them, to verify *one* facet. And this

H

picture is taken immediately from reality, for we say: "here is a chair" when we only see *one* side of it. (. . .)

'The phenomenon is not a symptom for something else which first makes the proposition true or false, but it is itself what verifies the proposition' (PR 225).

Do we say, for example, that we have certain feelings of dampness and cold, or a definite visual impression, and that we take this as a symptom or a criterion that it will rain? Do we get information about whether it is raining if we perceive rain? Or do we once again only get information about this information? What is this information as information about something in general supposed to characterize? Does my eye give me information about the fact that there is a chair there (see PI 354, 356)?

147   It is the concern of physics to furnish explanations and to establish regularities. Physics, accordingly, does not offer a description of the structure of states of affairs as they are phenomenologically presented. Phenomenology, on the contrary, wants to discover and understand the sense of the world. Before we can establish whether something is true or false we first of all have to find out its sense. Sense (*Sinn*) is, therefore, possibility (see w, p. 63). Phenomenology deals with possibility, that is, with the sense, on the basis of which truth and falsity are themselves possibilities.

148   All our forms of speech are derived from the normal physical language and are poorly used in phenomenology. Indeed, the most annoying errors always arise when one wants to describe the immediately given with these speech forms. We therefore have to make our way carefully and circumspectly if we want to describe reality as it is really given.

Reality is given to us in language. If we show what is essential to language then we *eo ipso* immediately represent the immediate experience. The question, therefore, is to separate what is essential to our language from what is inessential.

'The phenomenological language or "primary language" as I called it, does not now appear before me as a goal; I now no longer hold it to be necesary. All that is possible and necessary is to distinguish the essential from the inessential in our language.

'That is, if one describes, as it were, the class of languages which fulfil their goal, then with that one has shown what is essential to them and immediately represented the immediate experience.

'Every time I say that one could replace such and such a representation through certain others, we take a step forward towards the goal of grasping the essence of what is represented.

'A knowledge of what is essential in our language and what is inessential for the purpose of representation, a knowledge of what parts of our language are idling wheels, amounts to the construction of a phenomenological language' (PR 1).

The essence of language lies in our everyday language. By means of it we can describe phenomena. Phenomenological language is found, therefore, in our everyday language (see W, p. 45). In phenomenology one is speaking only about something that is really perceptible and not about hypothetical objects (see PR 218).

149 The descriptions of phenomena by means of an hypothesis or of the network proper to the world of bodies intrudes by reason of its simplicity into the infinitely complicated phenomenological description (see PR 230).

There are snags in such a procedure. Where a description that arises from an hypothesis suggests a body and there is none: there, we should like to say, is a *spirit* (see PI 36). And by 'spirit' we often imagine a gaseous, ethereal object. As long as we treat that as a raw hypothesis, as an auxiliary construction, it is not dangerous; it only becomes dangerous when we take talk about a spirit seriously and then think of this as a, even if sublimated, body.

'As long as one imagines by soul a thing or a body that is in the head, this hypothesis is *not* dangerous. The danger does not lie in the incompleteness and rawness of our models but in their lack of clarity (obscurity).

'The danger begins when we notice that the old model is not satisfactory, but do not alter it, but only, as it were, sublimate it. As long as I say that the thought is in my head everything is in order; it becomes dangerous when we say that the thought is not in my head but in my mind' (PR 230).

150 A similar mistake, for example, lies in our thinking of time as some sort of *special thing* (see BB, p. 6). The danger of wanting to see things more simply or other than they are persists in the highest degree. Phenomenology must describe things in their complexity as well as in their specific character. It has to take them as they are. It may not want to understand them as something else than what they are given as.

'Is the flame puzzling because it is ungraspable? Indeed – but why does that make it puzzling? Why should the ungraspable be more puzzling than what is graspable? Unless because we *want* to grasp it' (z 126).

H

COMPLEX AND THING

I

151   The world is our fundamental system. We understand the world in a global manner. But within the world we make distinctions. Without distinctions there is nothing. If the world consisted of only one thing, then there would not even be *one* thing. If there were only *one* substance then one would have no use for the word 'substance'. 'The concept of "substance" presupposes the concept "distinction of substance", . . . just as the concept of *colour* presupposes the distinction between *colours*". (z 353). If there is only a single thing there is nothing. If there were only one colour there would be no such thing as colour. 'If, for example, someone his whole life long had seen only red – would he then not say that he knows only one colour? In such a case one has to say: if everything he sees were red and if he could describe it, then he would also have to be able to construct the sentence: "that is not red" and this presupposes already the existence of other colours. Or he means by that something he cannot describe. He then does not know at all a colour in our sense, and then it is also not possible to *ask* whether red presupposes a system of colours. If, therefore, the word "red" has a meaning, it already presupposes a system of colours' (w, p. 261).

If something is contrasted with nothing, then I cannot contrast it. Only when it is distinguished by something, when it is other than something else, can I grasp it at all (see т 2.0231).

Only in a system in which I can make distinctions, distinctions, that is to say, which belong to the system, can I form propositions at all. What is essential in a proposition is that it is a picture and that it is compound. Let us now take as example

the proposition: 'this is yellow'. In this case I have to be able
to distinguish 'this' from 'yellow' and 'yellow' from 'red', and
so forth. I have to be able to recognize 'this' even if it is red.
If there were no colours, if there were only 'yellow', if 'this' and
'yellow' formed a unity, they could be represented by only *one*
symbol, and we would not have a proposition (see w, pp. 90,
97).

152   With the problem of the world and of the distinctions in
it we once more come against the problem of infinity and of
infinite divisibility.

That there is an extended visual space for me stems from
there being distinctions in this visual space. The problem of
infinite division is prefigured in the problem of the smallest
visible distinction. Our visual field is continuous, as the world as
a whole is continuous, and the smallest visible difference
appears on the one hand to contradict continuity and, on the
other hand, it has to be able to be connected with it.

If I make a series of visual distinctions, produce, therefore,
discontinuity, then a continuity is produced if these distinctions
are no longer visible, but merge into one another. But distinction breaks up continuity! But in such a way that the discontinuity of the smallest distinction first makes the continuous
space visible at all. That means that there is no contradiction
here, that continuity in our visual field consists in our *seeing* no
discontinuity (see PR 136, 137). Without distinctions we do not
see continuity. Therefore, we do not see the discontinuity which
makes the continuity visible to us.

153   By my making distinctions in the world it becomes
evident that the world is complex. But precisely because it is
complex and because I can make distinctions there have to be
simple things, as it were, the ultimate term of the process of
distinguishing.

Nevertheless, it is difficult to come upon these simple things.
'As examples of something simple I always think of points of
the visual field. (Just as parts of the visual field always come to
mind as typically composite objects)' (NB, p. 45). But is a point
in our visual field really a simple object, a thing? What evidence
could decide such a question (see NB, p. 3)?

If we want to pursue the question of the simple thing, then we have to ask: 'out of what component parts, then, is reality composed?' The notions 'simple' and 'composite' belong together. Nevertheless, we then see that the word 'simple' can have an immense number of interrelated meanings. Indeed, soon the questions about the simple appear to us as absurd (see NB, p. 45), and in such a way that they appear as if they could never be decided at all. 'But what are the simple constituent parts of which reality is composed? – What are the simple constituent parts of a chair? – The bits of wood of which it is made? Or the molecules, or the atoms? – "Simple" means: not composite. And here the point is: in what sense "composite"? It makes no sense at all to speak absolutely of the "simple parts of a chair".

'Again: Does my visual image of this tree, of this chair, consist in parts? And what are its simple component parts? Multi-colouredness is one kind of complexity; another is, for example, that of a broken outline composed of straight bits. And a curve can be said to be composed of an ascending and a descending segment.

'If I tell someone without any further explanation: "What I see before me now is composite", he will have the right to ask: "What do you mean by 'composite'? For there are all sorts of things that that can mean!" – The question "Is what you see composite?" makes good sense if it is already established what kind of complexity – that is, which particular use of the word – is in question. If it had been laid down that the visual image of a tree was to be called "composite", if one saw not just a single trunk, but also branches, then the question "Is the visual image of this tree simple or composite?", and the question "What are its simple component parts?", would have a clear sense – a clear use. And of course the answer to the second question is not "the branches" (that would be an answer to the *grammatical* question: "What are here called 'simple component parts'?") but rather a description of the individual branches.

'But isn't a chessboard, for instance, obviously, and absolutely, composite? – You are probably thinking of the composition out of thirty-two white and thirty-two black squares. But could we not also say, for instance, that it was composed of the colours black and white and the schema of squares? And

if there are quite different ways of looking at it, do you still
want to say that the chessboard is absolutely "composite"?
– Asking "Is this object composite?" *outside* a particular
language-game is like what a boy once did, who had to say
whether the verbs in certain sentences were in the active or
passive voice, and who racked his brains over the question
whether the verb "to sleep" meant something active or passive.

'We use the word "composite" (and therefore the word
"simple") in an enormous number of different and differently
related ways. (Is the colour of a square on a chessboard simple,
or does it consist of pure white and pure yellow? And is white
simple, or does it consist of the colours of the rainbow? – Is this
length of 2 cm simple, or does it consist of two parts, each 1 cm
long? But why not of one bit 3 cm long, and one bit 1 cm long
measured in the opposite direction?)' (PI 47).

154   If we also do not get to know simple objects by intuition,
nevertheless we do know complex objects. We know from
intuition that they are complex. Do they not have to be
made up of simple things (see NB, p. 50)? And is it not true
that if we could say 'this', then we have a simple object before
us?

'It seems that the idea of a *simple* is already contained in that
of a complex and in the idea of analysis, such that, completely
abstracting from any sort of examples of simple objects or of
propositions in which one is talking about such objects, we
arrive at this idea and see (*einsehen*) the existence of simple
objects as a logical necessity – *a priori*.

'It seems that the existence of simple objects is related to that
of complex objects in the way that the sense of −p is related to
the sense of p. The *simple* object is presupposed in the complex
one (. . .).

'What seems to us given *a priori* is the concept: *this*. – This
is identical with the concept of an *object*' (NB, pp. 60f).

II

155   But if 'this' is given to us as identical with the concept of
an object, it seems as if all objects would be, in a certain sense,

simple objects. If, for example, a simple name denotes an object which seems to us to be infinitely complex, then that can lead us to establishing that this object has its own definiteness, and therefore is indeed simple. For example, surfaces in our visual field can be simple objects in that we do not perceive a single point of these surfaces separately. In the case of visual images of stars this even appears to be certain (see NB, p. 64).

Do we now perhaps have to even go so far as to ask: are there, therefore, really no complex objects, but are, in a certain sense, all names genuine names and all objects simple objects (see NB, p. 61)?

'We can even conceive a body apprehended as in movement, *and together with its movement*, as a thing. So the moon circling around the earth moves around the sun. Now here it seems clear that this reification (*Verdinglichung*) is nothing but a logical manipulation – though its possibility of this may be extremely significant.

'Or let us consider reifications like: a tune, a spoken sentence. –

'When I say "x" has reference, do I have the feeling: it is impossible that "x" should stand for, say, this knife or this letter? Not at all. On the contrary.

'A complex just is a thing!' (NB, p. 49.)

156 The name brings the complex reference of complexes together into unity (see NB, p. 71). The complex then functions as a simple object; its compositeness becomes indifferent to us and disappears from view.

But it always appears as if there were composite objects which function as simple objects, something which one could treat as a thing, and really simple things at that (see NB, p. 69; p. 43)!

That a name denotes a complex object one gathers from the indefiniteness of the sentences in which it appears. This indefiniteness stems from the universality of the denoted complexes which now are more closely determined, that is, the name has to be analysed with regard to what it contains (see NB, p. 69).

There exists surely a process of analysis. And what will be the end of the analysis (see NB, p. 46)?

If I can make distinctions then I have to be able to repeat these processes of distinguishing. If I can form an image then

I have to be able to repeat these processes of forming the image. If there are complexes, then I have to be able to break them down; then there must be permanent elements, for otherwise I am at sea and there is no longer anything definite. I need simple things because I need determinateness. Without determinateness of sense there is no sense at all. Therefore, simplicity appears to us as the possibility of truth.

'Is it, *a priori*, clear that in analysing we must arrive at simple components – is this, e.g., involved in the concept of analysis –, or is analysis *ad infinitum* possible? – Or is there in the end even a third possibility? (. . .)

'And it keeps on forcing itself upon us that there is some simple indivisible, an element of being, in brief, a thing.

'It does not go against our feeling that *we* cannot analyse *propositions* so far as to mention the elements by name; no, we feel that the *world* must consist of elements. And it appears as if that were identical with the proposition that the world must be what it is, it must be definite. Or in other words, what vacillates is our determinations, not the world. It looks as if to deny things were so much as to say that the world can, as it were, be indefinite in some such sense as that in which our knowledge is uncertain and indefinite.

'The world has a fixed structure. (. . .)

'And these parts are then actually indivisible, for further divided they just would not be *these*. (. . .)

'The demand for simple things *is* the demand for definiteness of sense' (NB, pp. 62–3). 'Mankind has always sought for a science in which the simple is the sign of truth' (NB, p. 83).

157   What constitutes a thing is the fixed, the subsisting, the definite. Over against every other thing it is characterized by its independence. Still, this independence is at the same time a form of dependence, in as much as things are connected with one another. Things in their definiteness and independence point from themselves to other things in their independence, just like links on a chain.

'Things are independent in so far as they can occur in all *possible* situations, but this form of independence is a form of connection with states of affairs, a form of dependence' (T 2.0122).

'Objects, the unalterable, and the subsistent are one and the same' (T 2.027).

'Objects are what is unalterable and subsistent; their configuration is what is changing and unstable' (T 2.0271).

'The configuration of objects produces states of affairs' (T 2.0272).

'In a state of affairs objects fit into one another like the links of a chain' (T 2.03).

'In a state of affairs objects stand in a determinate relation to one another' (T 2.031).

Since we need the unalterable, we do not get along without names. They are essential to the assertion that *this* thing has *that* property, and so forth (see NB, p. 53; PI 59).

III

158   We have now arrived at a point where we must again ask ourselves the question about simple objects. Apparently they are not objects in the usual sense. What then are objects? Are they something thing-like or something property-like, or are they relations?

There are elements to which we must be able to return again and again. We do not just come upon them but we come upon them as what underlies our representations. What is itself presented in our representations and through which something else is represented are the elements of the representation: the, so to speak, simple objects. That is, they are all elements having equal weight which are represented and with which something else lets itself be represented. If we say that every colour statement, for example, can be made with the help of four primary colours, then the four primary colours are elements of the representation (see w, p. 43).

This also shows that the object behaves differently than the element of a state of affairs (see w, p. 257). 'What I formerly called "objects", the simple, is simply what I can describe without having to be afraid that it perhaps does not exist; that is, that for which there is not existence and non-existence, and that means that about which we can speak *no matter what the case is*' (PR 36).

We infer the existence of simple objects by a process of analysis, of description, which as a result shows us what describes but can no longer be described; something that underlies all denotation and representation (see NB, p. 50; PG, p. 208).

'Every description presupposes that there is something unalterable in the world, something that is independent of the subsisting or non-subsisting of states of affairs. The elements are just this unalterable something. That there are simple elements is not the result of an abstract theory, but all of us have to fundamentally know it. And that is in agreement with our natural feeling. I can describe the table by the colours red, yellow, etc. Can my knowledge of colours change in the course of experience? Does it make any sense to say: "the more often I have seen the colour red the better I know its properties"? It is clear that here there is a kind of completeness of our knowledge. And that means: with reference to the elements we do not have anything else to learn.

'(We learn, to be sure, also the colours through experience. But this is not the experience of a state of affairs)' (w, p. 253).

IV

159 Objects as elements of a representation set up in every case a specific logical space.

'When I say: "I do not have a stomach ache' that presupposes already the possibility of a state of stomach aches. My present state and the state of a stomach ache lie, as it were, in the same logical space. (As when I say: I have no money. This statement already presupposes the possibility that I do indeed have money. It points to the null-point of the money-space.) The negative proposition presupposes the positive one and vice versa' (w, p. 67).

Only in this way can I describe something by alluding to something which is not. What I am alluding to has to be in the same space; otherwise there is no connection. That my present situation has nothing to do with a painful one makes sense, just as it makes no sense if I were to say that this rose has nothing to do with the conquest of Gaul by Caesar (see PR 82).

If I understand a question I understand the logical space in which it is asked (see w, p. 167).

160   Logical space is polarized. Everything found in it is always characterized by a 'more' or 'less' in comparison to something else in it. Its null-point is also the null-point of a scale, of a measure, which I apply (see PR 82).

If someone in a party-game is looking for an object he does not really look for it in space, but in the logical space which is created by the words 'hot' and 'cold' (see w, p. 88).

If I make a determination, if I use a measure, then the whole measure and the whole logical space is also given. In this space I can immediately describe in positive propositions what I am seeing as what it is. But I can also immediately describe with negative propositions, which stand on the same level in the logical space as the positive ones, what is not, and therefore make reference just to it.

'I do not see red but I see *that the azalea is red*. In this sense I also see that it is not blue. Its blueness is not an inference arrived at after the visual fact, but I grasp it (the conclusion) immediately in the act of vision.

'Positive and negative propositions stand on one level. If I apply a measure then I know not only how long something is but also how long it is not. If I verify the positive proposition I thereby also falsify the negative proposition. The moment I know that the azalea is red I also know that it is not blue. The two things are inseparable. The conditions for the truth of a proposition presuppose the conditions for its falsity, and vice versa' (w, p. 87).

161   Since everything is polarized in logical space, everything can also be other (than it is) under the condition that it remains in the same space. If under this condition everything can also be other than it is, then we also, so to speak, turn the condition around and say that only that really is which can also be other than it is.

162   Question: are then the words with which something is described in the same space as what is described?

'That the measure has to be, and is, in the same space as the measured object is intelligible. But to what degree are the *words* in the same space as the object whose length is described in words, or in the same space as a colour, etc.? It sounds absurd' (PR 45).

The presupposition of the sense of a proposition is to be reckoned as belonging to language. The measure of the measure (*Mass des Maßstabs*) belongs to the symbolism. 'The characteristic element of propositions of the sort "this is . . ." is only that in some way reality outside of the so-called sign-system enters into the symbol' (PR 95).

163   The elements which are together in a logical space, as, for example, the colours, have an elementary relationship to one another (see PR 76). Together these elements form a system (see PR 76). There is something arbitrary as well as non-arbitrary in this system (see z 357, 358). Logical space has something arbitrary because it is created with an eye towards reality which comes from us. It has something non-arbitrary because in it *reality* is seen. Logical space is what is common to reality and the system of propositions which expresses it. In it reality is joined with a system of propositions.

164   If I discover the inner unity of two systems, then this discovery would not be the same space or in the same spaces as the systems themselves. For otherwise there would have been no discovery. Such a discovery creates a new space. But it does not fill up some pre-existing hole. 'Where now an inner unity is known which formerly was not known, there was not previously an open place, an incompleteness, which is now filled out! –

'(One could not say at that time: "as far as I know the matter, from this point on I no longer know it")' (PR 158).

V

165   The logical spaces give us to some extent different, separate perspectives on reality. They are enclosed by overlapping similarities. Similarity is the fundamental element of reality. In it is shown that we understand reality as a whole

(*im ganzen*). Without it we could not compare anything to anything else; we could give no examples. It is the foundation of family-resemblance. In it the elements of a representation are joined together; they are to some extent inherent in one another. By it no indefiniteness is carried into our understanding. But it shows us that understanding and saying rest basically upon similarity. They are fundamentally metaphorical.

Let us take an example: someone knows the use of the words 'light' and 'dark' and I say to him that he is supposed to put an arbitrary set of objects in rows according to their brightness. He then constructs a row of books and other objects and then he writes in addition the series 'i, e, a, o, u'. If I ask him why he has done that he answers: 'i is certainly brighter than e, and e is brighter than a' and so forth. Perhaps I say to him that i is certainly not brighter than e in the way that this book is brighter than that one. Perhaps I also ask him whether the vowels perchance have produced in him colour representations and whether he then perhaps puts these colour representations in order. He only shrugs his shoulders and says: 'But i *is* brighter than e, and so on' (see BB, pp. 139, 134).

Another example: for many people the individual days of the week are 'skinny' or 'fat' (see PI, pp. 216f; BB, p. 137).

And still another example: 'We say we experience tension and relaxation, relief, strain and rest in cases as different as these: A man holds a weight with outstretched arm; his arm, his whole body is in a state of tension. We let him put down the weight, the tension relaxes. A man runs, then rests. He thinks hard about the solution of a problem in Euclid, then finds it, and relaxes. He tries to remember a name, and relaxes on finding it' (BB, p. 129).

166 Once similarity is seen, then a problem arises precisely because one is concerned not with identity but with similarity. We then ask ourselves what really constitutes similarity. What allows us to say that the various cases we just enumerated are cases of tension and relaxation? 'What makes us use the expression "seeking in our memory", when we try to remember a word? Let us ask the question "What is the similarity between looking for a word in your memory and, for example, looking for a book on a shelf?"' (BB, p. 129.) Or a friend in the park?

167 How are we tempted to answer this question? A first answer appears to lie in the establishing of connecting – or intermediate links, of interpolated cases. 'One might say that the case which looking in your memory is most similar to is not that of looking for a friend in the park, but, say, that of looking up the spelling of a word in a dictionary. And one might go on interpolating cases' (BB, p. 129).

168 A second answer appears to lie in the derivation of genuine common elements. If I am looking for a word in my memory or if I am looking up its correct spelling in a dictionary, then it fits both cases that at first I was not able to write the word and then I could write it. We call this the derivation of common characteristics. This answer is untenable.

We do not need to be conscious of the similarity, and for the most part we also are not. In other words: it is not the similarity which strikes us but the expression has simply forced itself upon us.

'One might be inclined to say: "Surely a similarity must strike us, or we shouldn't be moved to use the same word." – Compare that statement with this: 'A similarity between these cases must strike us in order that we should be inclined to use the same picture to represent both." This says that some act must precede the act of using this picture. But why shouldn't what we call "the similarity striking us" consist partially or wholly in our using the same picture? And why shouldn't it consist partially or wholly in our being prompted to use the same phrase?

'We say: "This picture (or this phrase) suggests itself to us irresistibly.' Well, isn't this an experience?' (BB, pp. 129–30.)

There is here neither an intermediate level nor an antecedent establishment of similarity, but this experience is immediate.

The case of similarity is just like other cases with which the grammar of a word seems to suggest to us a certain necessity of intermediate levels or preparatory acts. *De facto* it is otherwise. I neither have to understand an order before carrying it out; nor do I have to show where my pain is before I can point to it; nor do I have to know a melody before I can sing it; and also the similarity does not have to have struck me before I express it.

Let us take one more case in which there is something really common. For example, two pictures of landscapes in which the same bush is found. These two pictures have the bush as a common element. Or in two piles of tools there is a crowbar as the common element (see BB, p. 130). But the common elements have nothing to do in fact with the similarity of the pictures or the piles themselves; they do not ground the similarity.

To take another case, if we say that 'we also meant something by "strain" which was common to mental and bodily strain, then it would be false to say that they are both called "strain" because they resemble one another and one would have to say: they are called "strain" because there is strain present in both' (BB, p. 134).

Another case is the one in which I consider two faces and say that they resemble one another. After some time I establish that I now know in what the resemblance consists which I previously only noticed in a general sort of way and I say: it's the eyes. They have the same form! Then it is no longer really a question of a semblance between two faces but between two pairs of eyes (see BB, p. 136).

169 We see, therefore, that no common element grounds resemblance. How does it now stand with that common element which is supposed to bring the resemblance about? It is the resemblance itself.

' "Why do you call 'strain' all these different experiences?" – "Because they have some elements in common." – "What is it that bodily and mental strain have in common?" – "I don't know, but obviously there is some similarity." '

'Then why did you say the experiences had something in common? Didn't this expression just compare the present case with those cases in which we primarily say that two experiences have something in common? (Thus we might say that some experiences of joy and of fear have the feeling of heart-beat in common.) But when you say that the two experiences of strain had something in common, these were only different words for saying that they were similar. It was then no explanation to say that the similarity consisted in the occurrence of a common element' (BB, p. 132).

170 Resemblance, however, does not rest upon a transferred

I

or metaphorical meaning. If I were to be asked, for example, what I mean by a 'fat' and a 'lean' day, then I would have to explain the meaning of fat and lean in a completely normal way. I could not explain them with the aid of the example of Tuesday and Wednesday. For this reason one could speak here of 'primary' and 'secondary' meaning. Secondary meaning would be a meaning which a word has without the meaning's being able to be shown primarily in the case of the word itself.

But that has nothing to do with the fact that resemblance would not be immediate without a kind of transfer, which again would be a kind of connecting link or intermediate level. 'The secondary sense is not a "metaphorical" sense. If I say: "For me the vowel e is yellow" I do not mean "yellow" in a metaphorical sense, – for I could not express what I want to say in any other way than by means of the idea "yellow" ' (PI 216).

Resemblance is immediate and ultimate, without intermediate steps, without *tertium comparationis*. 'If someone said: "I do see a certain similarity here, only I can't describe it", I should say: "This itself characterizes your experience" ' (BB, p. 136).

I

MEANING, AS, LANGUAGE-GAME

I

171 Objects in the usual sense, the individual thing we find in the world, seem to be denoted by words. These words have a meaning and indeed it seems as if the meaning of these words were nothing other than the objects which they denote or signify. If that were so, then in our investigation of the relation of word and object we could discover how the individual thing is connected with the world and with language.

172 'Cum ipsi (majores homines) appellabant rem aliquam, et cum secundum eam vocem corpus ad aliquid movebant, videbam, et tenebam hoc ab eis vocari rem illam, quod sonabant, cum eam vellent ostendere. Hoc autem eos velle ex motu corporis aperiebatur: tamquam verbis naturalibus omnium gentium, quae fiunt vultu et nutu oculorum, ceterorumque membrorum actu, et sonitu vocis indicante affectionem animi in petendis, habendis, rejiciendis, fugiendisve rebus. Ita verba in variis sententiis locis suis posita, et crebro audita, quarum rerum signa essent, paulatim colligebam, measque jam voluntates, edomito in eis signis ore, per haec enuntiabam (Augustine, *Confessions*, I, 8). '[When they (my elders) named some object, and accordingly moved towards something, I saw this and I grasped that the thing was called by the sound they uttered when they meant to point it out. Their intention was shown by their bodily movements, as it were the natural language of all peoples: the expression of the face, the play of the eyes, the movement of other parts of the body, and the tone of voice which expresses our state of mind in seeking, having, rejecting or avoiding something. Thus, as I heard words repeatedly used

in their proper places in various sentences, I gradually learned to understand what objects they signified; and after I had trained my mouth to form these signs, I used them to express my own desires.]

'These words, it seems to me, give us a particular picture of the essence of human language. It is this: the individual words in language name objects – sentences are combinations of such names. – In this picture of language we find the roots of the following idea: Every word has a meaning. This meaning is correlated with the word. It is the object for which the word stands' (PI 1).

173   What is essential in this conception, therefore, is that the words signify something, *name* them. But what do they signify? In general, if we say that all words of a language signify something, then with that nothing has yet been said. The expression is too vague and general. 'Imagine someone's saying: "*All* tools serve to modify something. Thus the hammer modifies the position of the nail, the saw the shape of the board, and so on." – And what is modified by the rule, the glue-pot, the nails? – "Our knowledge of a thing's length, the temperature of the glue, and the solidity of the box." – Would anything be gained by this assimilation of expression? –

'The word "signify" is perhaps used in the most straightforward way when the object signified is marked with the sign (. . .).

"It is in this and more or less similar ways that a name means and is given to a thing. – It will often prove useful in philosophy to say to ourselves: naming something is like attaching a label to a thing' (PI 14, 15).

174   The expression 'to name, to signify' not only says nothing because it is too general but it is false if it is generally taken for how words function in language.

We only need to ask ourselves: How does a word 'signify', That is, how do we learn what it signifies? One will answer: by ostensive teaching, by an ostensive explanation (see PI 6).

Before we ask how ostensive teaching is supposed to function, we have to ask ourselves: is 'naming' all that words do?

'One thinks that learning language consists in giving names

to objects. Viz., to human beings, to shapes, to colours, to pains, to moods, to numbers, etc. To repeat – naming is something like attaching a label to a thing. One can say that this is preparatory to the use of a word. But *what* is it a preparation *for*?

' "We name things and then we can talk about them: can refer to them in talk." – –As if what we did next were given with the mere act of naming. As if there were only one thing called "talking about a thing". Whereas in fact we do the most various things with our sentences. Think of exclamations alone, with their completely different functions. Water! Away! Ow! Help! Fine! No! – Are you inclined still to call these words "names of objects"?' (PI 26, 27.)

175   And now how is ostensive explanation supposed to function? Let us assume that I want to explain the number '2' to someone and point to two nuts. But the one to whom I give this definition can assume that by the word 'two' I mean this group of nuts. Or, if I want to explain to him ostensively the words "those are nuts", then he can assume that I am meaning the number "two" by that.

Perhaps someone says: two has to be defined in such a way that one says, this *number* is called two. But then the word 'number' has to have already been explained and understood (see PI 29).

Ostensive definition, therefore, explains the meaning if it is already clear in advance how the word is to be used. (see PI 30). There can, therefore, be no talk of naming or signifying on the basis of ostension.

How strongly ostensive definition depends on the previous clarification of the use of a word we can make clear to us by means of the following example:

'Let us then explain the word "tove" by pointing to a pencil and saying "this is tove" (. . .) The definition can then be interpreted to mean:

> This is a pencil
> This is round
> This is wood
> This is one
> This is hard, etc., etc.' (BB, p. 2).

Here it is clear that the definition is completely dependent upon the role which the word is supposed to play in language. Pointing is of no use here.

176   Pointing, ostensive explanation, can be understood as the translation from a gestural language into a word language. If I point to an object and say: 'That is "violet" ', then I have to already know what a colour is and what the name of the colour is (see PG 45).

177   It is the same as when I try to make a language intelligible to some other person. This already presupposes a language. That also shows us that we cannot learn a language *through* a language. We learn a language just by learning it, but not through a language which would be external to it. We do not make our way out of language.

"If I explain to a person the meaning of a word "A" by saying "this is A" and pointing to something, this expression can be meant in two ways. Either it is itself already a sentence and can then only be understood if the meaning of A is already known. That is, I can only leave it to chance whether or not the other person understands the sentence in the way I mean it. Or the sentence is a definition. I would have, perhaps, said to someone: "A is ill", but he did not know whom I meant by A and now I pointed to a man and said: "this is A."

'Now the expression is a definition, but this can only be understood if the kind of object is already known through the grammatically understood sentence "A is ill." That means, however, that every sort of making intelligible of a language already presupposes a language. And in a certain sense the use of a language is not to be taught. That is, not to be taught by language, just as one cannot learn, say, piano-playing by language. – That means nothing more than that I cannot get out of language by means of language' (PR 6).

178   The person who comes to a foreign country will sometimes be able to learn the language of the inhabitants by ostensive explanations, for he is already in possession of a language. Augustine's idea corresponds to such a situation, which, therefore, presents a simpler thing than the original learning of a language.

'And now, I think, we can say Augustine describes the learning of human language as if the child came into a strange country and did not understand the language of the country (. . .). Or again: as if the child could already *think*, only not yet speak' (PI 32).

When Augustine speaks about the learning of language the process of naming appears for him to be the be-all and end-all of language. 'One could also say, Augustine represents the matter too simply; or again; he represents a simpler matter' (PG 19).

179 Augustine is thinking first of all and mainly of nouns and is not talking about a difference in kinds of words. In this connection he forgets that words, even if they appear identical in writing and sound, nevertheless have various functions. We see the uniformity of words, however, in fact only in a language that is foreign to us. 'Not' and 'table' and 'green' are then for us things of the same sort. In a language in which we are fluent we look right through the sound and written image, so to say, and experience immediately the words of the various word-kinds in a totally different manner. One can compare with this the various lines having various functions on a map. 'The tyro sees a mass of lines and does not know the variety of their meanings' (PG 21).

In their external resemblance and in the inner variety of their functions it is possible to compare words in a certain sense with the handles in the cab of a locomotive. 'Just as the handles in the cab of a locomotive have various kinds of use, so do the words of a language, which in a certain sense resemble handles. One is the handle of a crank; it can be continually adjusted, for it operates a valve; another activates a switch which has two positions; a third is the handle of a pump and only works if it moved up and down; etc. But all look alike for they are grasped with the hand' (PG 20).

180 It has become clear in the meantime that the meaning of a word is not the object which it names or signifies, but the role it plays in the language. The meaning of a word lies in how it is used in the language, in how it is applied. 'One knows the meaning of a word when one knows how to use it' (w, p. 237).

181　We learn the meaning of a word by incorporating it into our language (see OC 61). This always happens under definite circumstances, but the describing of these circumstances does not belong to the meaning, and also not to the learning of the use of the word. The circumstances under which we learn a word belong to the praxis of life. In this way it also becomes clear that we do not first and foremost (*in erster Linie*) learn names. 'The child does not learn that there are books, a chair, etc., etc., but learns to fetch books, set himself on a chair, etc.' (OC 476). If, therefore, we interpret words as names, then we do not describe their use but we only give a meagre reference to such a description.

182　Even when we want to acknowledge a sign as a symbol that is, as a word, we have to advert to its meaningful use (see W, p. 167). If a sign is not applied, not used, then it is meaningless. That is the sense of Ockham's motto. What in a certain context is unnecessary has, therefore, no meaning in this context. (see T 3.326, 3.328, 5.47321). A sign that is not used drops out of its context as irrelevant (see PI 293).

183　I immediately know the use of a word, that is, its meaning, if I know it, or put otherwise: I immediately understand the meaning of a word if I know how it is used (see PG 28).

The use of a word follows rules, but I do not obey rules when I use it (see PI 292). Every well-known word in itself bears an atmosphere, a 'halo' of weakly intimated uses (see PI, p. 181).

184　Because what is essential in a word is its meaning, it is possible to replace one word by another which has the same meaning. 'With that a place is fixed for the word and it is possible to put one word in place of another, if one puts it in the same place.

'If I should decide (also in my thoughts) to say a new word instead of "red", how would it be shown that this new one stands in place of the word "red"?

'If it were agreed in English instead of "no" to say "non" and therefore instead of "red" to say "no", in this way the word "no" would remain in the language and still one could say that "non" is now used in the way that "no" was formerly, and that now "no" is used *in another way*' (PG 22).

I could even understand a piece of nonsense provided I had ascribed to it, within a system of linguistic acts, a place, provided I had given it a meaning (see PG 34).

185   What do I do, therefore, when I explain the meaning of a word? I explain the place and use of a word in language. The meaning of a word is, therefore, what the explanation of a word explains. The meaning is deposited in the explanation of the meaning. It explains the use of the word.

Since grammar describes the use of words in language, the location of the word in the grammar is its meaning (PG 23).

The explanation can eliminate differences of opinion with respect to a meaning (see PG 24). Since it explains the kind of use of a word, it also shows us at the same time what sort of word it is.

II

186   If we want to explain the meaning of a word, then we have to see clearly that this has nothing to do with the explanation of the goal or of the effect of a word. It can be replaceable in its effect by no other word, while various words can have the same meaning (see PG 32).

187   The criterion for knowing the meaning is not, however, the ability to give the rules of its use. 'What is the sign that someone understands a game? Does he have to be able to recite the rules? Is it not also a criterion that he can play the game, that is, he just plays, and would it not be possible for him, if asked about the rules, to fall into embarrassment? (. . .)

'Indeed, just as the grammar of a language is first sketched and first appears when the language has been already spoken *for a long time* by men, primitive games are also played without their table of rules being laid out. Indeed, too, without a single rule having been formulated for it' (PG 26).

III

188   That the meaning of a word depends on its place and its use in language is important for the problem of the meaning of a name. The word 'meaning' is used in a way contrary to language if one thereby signifies the thing to which the word corresponds. The bearer of a name is not the meaning of the name (see PI 39, 40).

'The meaning of a name is not what we point to in the ostensive explanation of the name; that is, it is not the bearer of the name. – The expression "the bearer of the name 'N' " is synonymous with the name "N". The expression can be used in place of the name. "The bearer of the name 'N' is ill" means: N is ill. One does not say: the meaning of "N" is ill.

'The name does not lose its meaning if its bearer ceases to exist (if, for example, he dies)' (PG 27).

The meaning of a name is, therefore, determined through the rules of use of the name. These rules of use can be such that the name can also still be used when its bearer no longer exists. Because the name is not identical with the bearer of the name, the name also still has a meaning when its bearer no longer exists.

If I understand the meaning of a word then I understand precisely the role which it plays in the language.

189   How a word is understood, what meaning it has, words alone do not say (see z 144). It is subsumed into the usual actions, into a totality of rules, which are embedded in a comprehensive system, in a comprehensive form of life (see OC 229; W, p. 150; PR 152). Therefore, nothing may be isolated, nothing may be cut out.

'A coronation is the picture of pomp and dignity. Cut one minute of this proceeding out of its surroundings: the crown is being placed on the head of the king in his coronation robes. – But in different surroundings gold is the cheapest of metals, its gleam is thought vulgar. There the fabric of the robe is cheap to produce. A crown is a parody of a respectable hat. And so on' (PI 584).

190   That words alone do not say what the meaning of a word is has nothing to do with words being accompanied for us by representations, associations, and feelings. All these are not to be confused with the meaning. We can, for example, regularly have something like 'if-feelings', 'and-feelings', 'or-feelings', 'but-feelings'. These feelings can vary in their intensity or also be totally absent. They do not explain the words, for no matter how strong they are, or whether they are simply not there at all, the use of the word remains the same.

'Let us consider the following example: William James speaks somewhere of the fact that we join definite feelings to the words "if", "and", "not", that one could therefore speak of an "if-feeling". These feelings are supposed to explain the meanings of these words. – How does one arrive at the idea that there are such feelings? Well, someone utters a sentence, for example: "if it rains today, I can't go out", and observes what happens. If you do that you will immediately notice that the "if-feeling" is not always "equally strong". You are perhaps inclined to say that you utter the sentence at one time more mechanically and at another time less so. – But just think how you utter it when you use it in practice. For in practical use it surely fulfils its authentic function. You will see that you utter it differently on different occasions and that the that-feeling varies not just according to its force. Further: you will see that what you call this feeling is connected with a definite intonation, a gesture, a facial expression; if you change the intonation, the feeling is changed, for, at least partially, it is the feeling, the experience of this intonation. Perform the following experiment: say the if-sentence and make a *negative* movement of the head. If now we are not misled by a false conception of the grammar of the word "meaning" (*Bedeutung*) so that we believe there *must be* an if-feeling, we will say: there are if-feelings, namely, in the sense in which there are if-movements, and if-intonations. These things are characteristic for the use of the word "if", in so far as we often utter the word in this way. But they can also be completely absent and the word still be completely legitimately used' (*Eine Philosophische Betrachtung*, [Wittgenstein's reworking of the *Brown Book*], found in *Schriften* 5, p. 218).

191   Something similar is true of the feeling of conviction.

If we look for what corresponds to the experience of conviction
we will discover much that falls under it. As, for example, many
things can cause a face to make a friendly impression. What do
we want to name now as characteristic of the feeling of conviction? That plays no role, for it is irrelevant to the meaning of
the conviction which we are uttering (see BB, pp. 144–6).

192   The danger always exists that we will confuse the meaning with the mood which accompanies our use of the expression
instead of thinking of the praxis of its use. If we recite an
expression to ourselves in order to get to know the feeling which
it evokes in us, that is of no use to us here, for the feeling is not
its meaning (see OC 601).

Yes, but there is certainly something there which accompanies my words! On account of that I utter them. And this
something is what is important. To whom do we communicate
this, and how and on what occasion? 'The very fact that we
should so much like to say: "This is the important thing" –
while we point privately to the sensation – is enough to show
how much we are inclined to say, something which gives no
information' (PI 298).

IV

193   From the concept of meaning, as we have begun to set it
forth, we have to distinguish another one which we use when we
say, for example: that has a great or a deep meaning. If, for
example, I utter words with expression in reading, then they
seem to be completely filled with their meaning. But if by
meaning we understand the use of words, then that cannot be
(see PI, pp. 215f).

But is that correct? Isn't there really an affinity there? 'Is the
meaning then really only the use of the word? Is it not the way
this use engages with life' (PG 29)? Does there not also belong to
the meaning the individual use in concrete and specific situations into which it then penetrates at times in a special way,
and does it have a, supplementarily to some extent, special
meaning? And that would then be the meaning in the sense of
deep, important, and so on.

194   Because the use is part of our life this engaging is also called meaning and certainly has a relationship with the manner of application. But to avoid confusions we want to call this the goal of the word.

'We were saying: By the use we would not yet understand the *goal* of the word "perhaps". By goal, however, we meant here the role which it plays in human life. (And one could call this role the "meaning" of the word, in the sense in which one speaks of the "meaning of an event for our life".)

'But we were saying: by "meaning" we would understand what the explanation of the meaning explains. And the explanation of the meaning is no experimental proposition and no causal explanation, but rule, a convention.

'It would be possible to explain: the word "ha!" in our language has the goal of arousing alarm in the one spoken to. What does its having this goal reside in? What is the criterion for it? The word "goal", just like all words of our language, is used in various more or less related ways. Let us name two characteristic games: we could say the goal of an action is what is answered by an agent when asked about the goal.

'If, on the other hand, we say the hen clucks in order to call her chicks together, we infer this goal from the *effect* of the clucking. We would never call the gathering of the chicks the goal of the clucking if the clucking did not always, or for the most part, or under definitely specifiable circumstances, have this result. – One may now say that the goal, the effect of the word "ha!", is the most important thing about this word; but the explanation of the goal or of the effect is not what we call the explanation of the meaning.

'A word cannot, according to its effect, be replaced by another word; just as one cannot replace a gesture by another gesture. (A word has a *soul*, not just a meaning.) Also no one would believe that a poem remains *essentially unchanged* if one replaced its words by others according to corresponding conventions.

'We can interpret our statement "the meaning is what the explanation of the meaning explains" *in this way*: let us concern ourselves only with what is called the explanation of the meaning, and in no sense with meaning taken otherwise' (PG 32).

Certainly every word in various contexts can have a different character, a different aspect. But they are not correlates of the meaning. 'The meaning is not the experience of hearing or uttering the word, and the sense of the sentence is not the complex of these experiences' (PL, p. 181; see z 170).

What takes place in the use of words plays no role. Let us now assume that I say: 'Mr French is not French', in which the first 'French' is the proper name and the second signifies his nationality. In the case of the first 'French' there is certainly something different going on in my mind than in the case of the second. Good. I now try in the case of the first 'French' to think of the nationality and in the case of the second of the proper name. That strains me. And that also shows me that in the normal use of words I am not bringing their meaning to mind.

'If I say the sentence with this change of meanings, I feel that its sense disintegrates. – Now, it disintegrates *for me*, not for the other person to whom I am communicating. What harm does it do then?' (PI, p. 176.) When I use words there just does not occur that 'bringing to mind of the meaning' which I sometimes accomplish inwardly, for example, when I mix up the two meanings of 'French'.

V

195 Meaning is something inherently implicit, unexplicated. For example, if I hear a short melody and say: 'just consider its wealth of meanings' then that doesn't mean that in the act of listening I hear every one of those meanings separately. Meaning lies in the *flow* of thoughts and of life itself (see z 173). 'The conversation, the use, and the interpretation of words flow together and the word only has its meaning in the flow' (z 135). If I say, for example: 'he has departed', then the meaning is embedded in a complex situation, but I was not 'thinking' about it when I uttered the sentence. 'If a sensitive ear shows me, when I am playing this game, that I have now *this*, now *that* experience of the word – doesn't it also show me that I often do not have *any* experience of it in the course of talking? – For the fact that I then also mean it, intend it, now like *this* now like *that*, and maybe also say so later is, of course, not in question' (PI, pp. 215–16).

In this way I can understand a word all at once and this

understanding is something other than unfolding to myself the 'use' which is extended in time (see PI 138, 139, RFM I–130).

I can, therefore, know a meaning without having to describe it, indeed, often without being able to describe it. It is even possible that someone knows the meaning of a word exactly, that is, that he knows completely correctly how to use it and that, if he is supposed to describe the meaning, he does so in a completely false way. 'If I have learned to carry out a definite activity in a definite room (say, the cleaning of the room) and am in command of this technique, it still does not follow that I have to be prepared to describe the set-up of the room; even were I to notice immediately every alteration in it and also could describe it right away. (. . .)

'It would indeed be quite conceivable that someone knows his way around exactly in a city, that is, would find with certainty the shortest way from every place in the city to every other one, – and still be completely incapable of drawing a plan of the city. That, as soon as it tries it, he produces something *totally false*' (Z 119, 121).

VI

196   The same word can have various meanings. For example, we can use the word 'is' as a copula, as an equal sign, and as an expression of existence. Or in the sentence 'Green is green' the first word is a personal name and the last is an adjective (see T 3.323).

In the cases named here the change of meaning is clear. But the meaning of an expression and of a word can also fluctuate without one's noticing it. This is often very extensive. 'There is nothing more common than that the meaning of an expression varies in such a way that a phenomenon is now considered as a symptom and now as a criterion of a state of affairs. And then for the most part in such a case the change of meaning is not noticed. In science it is usual to turn phenomena which allow exact measurements into defining criteria of an expression; and one is then inclined to think that now the genuine meaning has been *found*. An enormous number of confusions arise in this way' (Z 438; see PI 79).

Or, for example, the number '1' can have a different meaning if one takes it at one time for a measure and another time for a number (see PI 533).

197   But it is not only the case that words have different meanings and that expressions vary, but the use of words is clearly prefigured only in normal cases.

The more abnormal the case is, the more dubious becomes what we really want to say (see PI 142). Moreover, many concepts are, as it were, only centres of variations for meanings which slide over into one another, which are only similar to one another (see BB, pp. 127ff; LAC, p. 32).

VII

198   I can choose what I want to mean. That is, I can choose my manner of expression, which, again, means that I choose a definite method of representation with which I establish a range of meanings (see W, pp. 162f). With that I determine what I understand, to wit, by grasping it as this and that, by grasping something as something. 'The question is: *what* do I get to know *as what*? For, "to know a thing as itself" means nothing' (PG 130). The range of what I grasp *as* something belongs to this thing itself. Therefore, one can, for example, 'say: "check if *that* is a circle" or "check whether *that* thing there is a hat." It is also possible to say: "see whether that is a circle or an ellipse", but not: ". . . whether that is a circle or a hat"; also not: "see whether that is a hat or red"' (PG, p. 206).

199   First of all, the *as* of the 'as something' is so implicit that, for example, I would not like to say: 'I see this *as* a face', but rather: 'I see it *so*' (see BB, pp. 170f). But in the *so* the *as* is already contained. For what seems to me to be one way can also seem to me to be otherwise, that is, *as* something else. That is to say, it is the same thing which appears to me now as this and on another occasion as something else (see BB, pp. 171f).

I can, therefore, see different aspects of the same thing, to some extent different as – structures. 'I consider a face, and all of a sudden notice its similarity with a different one. I *see* that it has not been altered; and yet I see it differently. This experience I call "the noticing of an aspect"' (PI, p. 193). That is, in choosing our manner of expression and our manner of representation – and we always do that – we interpret what we see and see what we interpret.

200 Although the 'as' is first of all implicit, it always impels us to set it in relief, to give expression to it, that is to say, in a fashion which is always still implicit. When, for example, we see a drawing which represents a face, then we would like to compare it with something which indeed does not exist, with an invisible paradigm with which it is supposed to agree, precisely because we see it *as* a face.

Or also, if we see a colour. It seems as if we would want to specify it, but not while we are saying something about it, but wanting to see it in relief from itself and to compare it with itself. 'You use it at the same time as the sample and as that which the sample is compared with' (BB, p. 174). What I see enters into my language like a sample because I see it as something (see BB, p. 175).

201 In three cases we have to consider the distinction between the 'constant seeing' of an aspect and the 'dawning of an aspect' (see PI, p. 194). It is the dawning of an aspect and the expression of a change of aspect as expression of a new perception along with the expression of the unchanged perception, which gives us the opportunity to make the 'as' explicit. Because the noticing disappears once again (see PI, p. 211), because what is noticed does not remain new, the explicit 'as' also again disappears. 'Ask yourself: for how long am I struck by a thing? How long is it *new* to me?

'In the aspect a physiognomy is present which passes away afterwards. It is almost as if there were a face there which I first *copy* and then perceive, without copying it' (PI, p. 210). The change of aspect or the dawning of an aspect evokes astonishment which the immediate recognition of it does not evoke (see PI, p. 199). 'I cause a theme to be repeated to myself and every time to be played in a slower tempo. Finally I say: "now it is right" or: "only *now* is it a march", "only now is it a dance." – In *this* tone is expressed the dawning of an aspect'

K

(PI, p. 206). In the change of aspect or in the dawning of an aspect we become aware of the 'as' and then we are able to represent something as something. 'To say: "I now see that as . . ." would have had for me just as little sense as on the occasion of seeing a knife and fork to say: "I see that now as a knife and fork." One would not understand this utterance. – Just as little as this: "This is now for me a fork" or: "that can also be a fork." '

'One also does not "*take*" what one knows as cutlery *for* cutlery; just as little as one, in eating, normally tries to move his mouth or aims at doing so'. (PI, p. 195). It is only by the dawning of a new aspect that we notice that we grasp something as something.

202   Because the 'as' is first and foremost implicit, we do not find it immediately in perception. ' "Seeing as . . ." does not belong to perception. And therefore it is like a seeing and again not like a seeing (. . .). And therefore the dawning of an aspect seems to be half a visual experience and half a process of thinking' (PI, p. 197).

203   The question is whether I really see something different every time or only interpret what I see in another way. The first alternative seems to fit. Why? Because seeing seems to be a *state*, since I see the thing in precisely *this* way, and because interpreting seems to be an *activity* of *thinking* and *acting*, since I already am doing something with the thing (see PI, p. 212). But it is not so simple. 'Is it introspection which teaches me whether I have to do with a genuine seeing or rather with an interpreting? First I have to get clear what I then would call an interpreting; by means of this one can learn whether something is to be called an interpreting or a seeing' (z 212).

Seeing and interpreting belong together. ' "A thought echoing in seeing" – one would like to say' (PI, p. 212). Interpretation does not force itself upon seeing, but rather is contained in it. 'But how is it possible that one *sees* something according to an *interpretation*? – The question represents it as a strange fact; as if here something were being forced into a form which really did not fit it. No squeezing, no forcing took place here' (PI, p. 200). If, therefore, we see something 'together', take different things together, seeing it as 'this', then that is a seeing which is determined by the concept, by interpretation (see PI, pp. 204, 208f).

We have to say, besides, that we do not see something according to an interpretation, for we do not relate it to an interpretation but according to an interpreting which itself is found in the activity of seeing (see Z 217). If we see a change of aspect then there takes place another activity of interpreting. We can then explicate this new interpreting as an interpretation. What we see is another aspect. If we grasp the change of aspect itself then we do not really see it but the change of interpretation (see Z 216).

204 There is also an interpreting which comes from uncertainty. 'Now can that be this way or that?' 'Well now, I interpret it this way' (see Z 208). This interpreting is not the one which determines seeing from the inside. Interpretative seeing is presupposed by a hesitant interpreting; but perhaps it is hesitant interpreting which leads us to the first form.

205 In the choice of a manner of expression and of representation, in the development of a seeing interpreting, in the development of the 'as' aspect, the logical space and the process of understanding are unfolded. 'Systems of communication ... we shall call "language-games". They are more or less akin to what in ordinary language we call games. Children are taught their native language by means of such games, and here they even have the entertaining character of games' (BB. p. 81).

Language-games, however, are not the fragments of a whole which is language itself (*der Sprache*) but we treat them as self-enclosed systems of understanding. That is, they are *in* language. In this way we can speak of a simple, primitive language sometimes as a language-game (see PI 7). To keep this point of view in mind, it very often is useful to imagine such a simple language to be the entire system of communication of a tribe in a primitive state of society (BB, p. 81).

206 We can also call special systems of understanding language-games. 'When the boy or grown-up learns what one might call special technical languages, e.g., the use of charts and diagrams, descriptive geometry, chemical symbolism, etc., he learns more language-games' (BB, p. 81).

207   Or we can think up clear and simple language-games which we want to use as objects of comparison, which, because of their similarity, throw a light on the relation of our language (see PI 130). 'The study of language-games is the study of primitive forms of language or primitive languages. If we want to study the problems of truth and falsehood, of the agreement and disagreement of propositions with reality, of the nature of assertion, assumption, and question, we shall with great advantage look at primitive forms of language in which these forms of thinking appear without the confusing background of highly complicated processes of thought. When we look at such simple forms of language the mental mist which seems to enshroud our ordinary use of language disappears. We see activities, reactions, which are clear-cut and transparent. On the other hand we recognize in these simpler processes forms of language not separated by a break from our more complicated ones. We see that we can build up the complicated forms from the primitive ones by gradually adding new forms.

'Now what makes it difficult for us to take this line of investigation is our craving for generality' (BB, p. 17).

208   Our calculi are often so constructed that they oppose something fixed (*etwas Festes*) to the fluctuating. The clearest example is mathematics and its idealization of reality.

'If we consider the real use of a word we see something in flux.

'To this fluctuating thing in our considerations we oppose something fixed. Similar to the way one paints a stable picture of a constantly altering image of a landscape.

'We are considering language *from the viewpoint* of a game played according to fixed rules. We are comparing it with this kind of game, we are measuring it by means of it.

'If, for our purposes, we want to subject the use of a word to definite rules, we put another use alongside of the fluctuating use by fixing in rules a characteristic aspect of the first use' (PG 36).

If one wanted to say: mathematics rests on the fact that we idealize reality, its properties, relations, and the like – in this way the first question would be: and what then becomes different through idealization?

209 Language-games as closed systems of understanding belong to *the* language-game, to the everyday language of adults. 'The picture we have of the language of the grown-up is that of a nebulous mass of language, his mother tongue, surrounded by discrete and more or less clear-cut language-games, the technical languages' (BB, p. 81).

Speaking does not exist for itself, as it were abstractly, but it is part of the praxis of life. 'The word "language-*game*" is supposed to emphasize here that the speaking of a language is part of an activity, or of a form of life' (PI 23). That is true also for the whole of language. 'I will also call the whole – consisting of language and the activities with which it is interwoven – the "language-game"' (PI 7).

210 Because in a language-game something is always grasped *as* something, because, therefore, it at least has an implicit as-structure, the language-game does not arise from a process of reflection, but we can reflect only within a language-game. For this reason a concept is at home in a language-game (see Z 391). In this way also systems of reasons can only be given within a language-game. 'The chains of reasons come to an end, to wit, on the boundary of the game' (PG 55). The language-game grounds at any given time the perspectives of an as-structure. Therefore, it does not itself have a ground. 'You must consider that the language-game, so to speak, is something unforeseen. I mean, it is not grounded. Not reasonable (or unreasonable).

'It stands there – like our life' (OC 559). The language-game gives to what is played in it its ground or reason. Because there are systems of grounds and of use only *in* a language-game, we can also establish:

'If the language-games are changed the concepts are changed and with the concepts, the meanings of the words' (OC 65).

VIII

211 'Language is for us a calculus; it is characterized by *language activities (Sprachhandlungen)*' (PG 140). Therefore we can also call language-games calculi. 'There exists between the way we use words in language and a calculus not perhaps a

mere analogy, but I can in fact understand the concept of a calculus in such a way that the use of words falls under it (. . .). What I do with the words of a language (in *understanding* them) is precisely the same thing that I do with the sign in a calculus: I operate with them. That I in one case carry out actions and in another case only write down the signs or cross them out, etc., makes no difference; for also what I do in a calculus is an action. *There is no sharp boundary here*' (w, pp. 168ff).

212   If the meaning of a word is its use, then we can also say that the meaning of a word is the way and manner that one performs calculations with it in a language-game. 'I said that the meaning of a word is the role it plays in a language calculus (I compared it to a piece in a game of chess). And let us now consider how a calculation is performed with a word, let us say, for example, the word "red". One states where the colour is found, what form or what size the spot or the body has which bears the colour, whether it is pure or mixed with other colours, is darker or brighter, remains the same or changes, etc., etc. Conclusions are drawn from the sentences, they are translated into images and into actions, one draws, measures, counts' (PG 31).

A calculus is determined by a fundamental assumption, therefore, by the perspective of an as-structure or of a context of proof. 'What functions as the ground of an assumption can be stated beforehand and determines a calculus; a system of transitions. Now if we inquire after a ground of this calculus we see that it is not on hand.

'Is the calculus, therefore, arbitrarily assumed by us? Just as little as fear of fire or of an angry man who is approaching us' (PG 68).

The fundamental assumption of a calculus or of a game determines its meaning. An alteration of the grammar of such a game actually leads us to another game, but not from something true to something false (see PG 68).

Fundamental assumptions are not arbitrary, but are connected with reality (see PG 111).

Because there are many closed systems of understanding, the meaning of a calculus is polyvalent (see w, p. 203).

J

RULE

213   Rules belong to games, and regularity belongs to language. What is a rule? First of all, we want to say that he who established rules according to which certain words are used and certain games are played, has not taken over the duty of giving an explanation of the word 'rule'. I can use the word 'rule' without first tabulating the rule for the use of this word. The rules which rule the word 'rule' are, moreover, not super-rules. They are nothing other than the explanation of the use of the word 'rule' (see PG 72).

214   But how do we use the word rule, that is, what is its meaning? It has various meanings. If, for example, we were to express what the rule says, then we could forego the word 'rule'. 'We say, for example: "that follows from this rule", but then we could cite the appropriate rule and in this way avoid the word "rule" ' (PG 73). That also proves to be true if we were to enumerate all rules of the game. Or we state fundamental rules and operations. Or we write down the rule-catalogue of a game. In this way we notice that we cannot, without more ado, state what is common to all these things which we group together with the word 'rule'. And then we establish that only in special cases does one need to delimit the rule from what is not the rule. In these cases it is easy to state the distinguishing characteristic. We can find an answer more easily if we ask: in opposition to what do we use it? We use, for example, the word 'rule' in opposition to 'word', 'illustration', and so on. In these cases a clear boundary can be drawn.

215   But we do not draw a clear boundary where we do not need it. Let us take as an example the word 'plant'. 'We can use

the word "plant" in an unmistakable way, but innumerable boundary cases can be constructed for which the decision whether something still falls under the concept of a "plant" would first have to be met. But is the meaning of the word "plant", therefore, in all other cases burdened with an uncertainty so that one could say that we use the word without understanding it? Indeed, would a definition which delimited this concept from several sides make clearer to us the meaning of the word in all sentences, would we, therefore, understand better all the sentences in which it appears?' (PG 73).

If we now ask how we have learned to understand anything at all, we discover: by examples. If I am asked about the meaning, then examples of usage occur to me. Exact boundaries cannot be drawn and also are not necessary (see PG 74, 75).

216   There exists a kinship between 'regular' and 'uniform', therefore, between 'rule' and 'same' (see PI 208, 225). If I want to teach someone a rule then I try to get him to continue in the same way as I have shown him. I point towards reality and say to him: 'continue in this way' or: 'and so forth'.

In this regard the words 'and so forth' have two functions. They first mean simply a series of further examples which clarify the rule for him. But they can also mean the infinity of the understanding which is grasped all at once with the conceiving of reality.

'We should distinguish between the "and so on" which is, and the "and so on" which is not, an abbreviated notation. "And so on ad inf." is *not* such an abbreviation. The fact that we cannot write down all the digits of π is not a human shortcoming, as mathematicians sometimes think.

'Teaching which is not meant to apply to anything but the examples given is different from that which "*points beyond*" them' (PI 208).

217   Yet 'same' does not mean 'the same'.

'Suppose someone gets the series of numbers 1, 3, 5, 7, . . . by working out the series $2x+1$. And now he asks himself: "But am I always doing the same thing, or something different every time?"'

'If from one day to the next you promise: "Tomorrow I will come and see you" – are you saying the same thing every day, or every day something different?' (PI 226.)

'Same' means: 'I make it equal to reality.' I act in agreement with reality, to wit, with an existent or an expected reality.

'The word "agreement" and the word "rule" are *related* to one another: they are cousins. If I teach anyone the use of one word, he learns the use of the other with it' (PI 224).

218   Because the rule rests on agreement it grounds an expectation. 'Grounded expectation is the expectation that a rule valid up to now will continue to be valid. For that purpose the rule has to be verified and its verification can, on its side, only be expected' (see PR 237; PG, p. 231). This demands repetition. 'It is not possible that there should have been only one occasion on which someone obeyed a rule (. . .). To obey a rule, to make a report, to give an order, to play a game of chess, are *customs* (uses, institutions)' (PI 199; see BB, p. 96). And recognition is proper to repetition (see OC 455).

Exception is a property of rules. If there were no exceptions there would also not be any rules. I can, to be sure, be in agreement with reality in various ways: I can see it in *this* way or *that*. Moreover, I do not follow a rule mechanically. If in following my rules I no longer am in agreement with reality, then I look for new rules which 'fit' better (see RFM V-8; PI 182). I can only determine a rule if I establish how long I will maintain it without reversing it. That is, I have to establish how many exceptions at the most I will allow (see PR 235).

219   The rule is a final element beyond which we cannot go. 'It is not possible to penetrate behind the rules, because there is no behind' (PG, p. 244). We do not first learn a rule which we then apply; it is given to us in the actual applying. 'If you demand a rule from which it follows that one cannot have miscalculated, the answer is that we have not learned this by a rule but by the fact that we have learned to calculate.

'The *essence* of calculating we have learned in learning to calculate.

'But can one not then describe how we convince ourselves of the reliability of a calculation? Of course! But in that case a

rule just does not appear. – The most important thing is: there is
no need of the rule. We are lacking nothing. We calculate
according to a rule, and that is enough' (see oc 44, 45, 46).

It is not an act of insight which, in the process of adding, lets
us apply the rule in such a way as we just apply it (see BB, p. 142).
We do not need to be always conscious of the direction
(*Winkes*) of a rule in order to do what it tells us. We just do it.
(see PI 223). 'Calculating prodigies who get the right answer but
cannot say how. Are we to say that they do not calculate?
(A family of cases)' (PI 236).

In a certain fashion we do not, therefore, 'need' the rule.
We do not notice it, and we do not understand it. 'Children
would have to be weighty philosophers in order to understand
the calculating taught in the primary school; lacking this they
need practice' (Z 703). The rule is practised.

Because we act according to a rule, checking what we 'regularly' do time and again yields only the same thing (see oc 77,
78, 459).

We apply the rule and we do so without a further rule. It is
not possible, that is, to apply a rule 'by means of' a rule, otherwise we would not be able to get off dead centre (see w, p. 155).

'What is "to learn a rule"? – *That*. What is "to make a
mistake in its application"? – *That*. And what is being pointed
to here is something indefinite' (oc 28).

220   There are rules which can never be spoken at all, which
only lie in the shadow, and precisely those are the most fundamental, because they are found apart from all doubt, in that
they are never put into question (see oc 87, 88).

The problem of the rule often first emerges when the rule has
to be put into question. 'The fundamental fact here is that we
lay down rules, a technique, for a game and that then when we
follow the rules, things do not turn out as we had assumed.
That we are, therefore, as it were entangled in our own rules'
(PI 125).

K

EXACTNESS AND VAGUENESS

I

221 We have shown that the meaning of a word lies in its use, in its role in a language-game, and that rules belong to a language-game. We have further seen that we can apply words and rules without having or being able to describe them. After we have spoken of rules we want now to emphasize the problem of exactness, vagueness, and so forth.

Rules are given immanently. They cannot be precisely defined. This leads to the problem of exactness, vagueness, and so on.

222 The normal use of the generic terms in language is vague. But they are completely usable and fulfil their purpose. Indeed, if I draw sharper boundaries, in this way I draw a picture sharply, where reality has smooth and gradual transitions. 'To believe they would be therefore unusable or yet not completely correspond to their purpose would be as if one wanted to say: "The heat which this oven gives off is of no use because one does not know where it begins and where it ends."'

'If, for the sake of explanation and to avoid misunderstandings in such a use of language, I want to draw sharp boundaries, these will be related to the flowing boundaries in our natural use of language the way sharp contours in a pen drawing are related to the gradual transitions of colour patches in the reality being represented' (PG 76). The pen drawing, however, is not the represented reality.

223 We can know something completely without, nevertheless, being able to say it. 'Compare *knowing* and *saying*:
　　　　how many feet high Mont Blanc is –

how the word "game" is used –
how a clarinet sounds.

If you are surprised that one can know something and not be able to say it, you are perhaps thinking of a case like the first. Certainly not of one like the third' (PI 78). Is to know 'something' perhaps some sort of equivalent of an unuttered definition (see PI 75)?

It is really not that, because we are not capable in most cases of stating rules of usage or of definitions when we are asked about them. And there is a good reason for that. The incapacity does not lie with us but in the fact that our concepts have no real definition. 'We are unable clearly to circumscribe the concepts we use; not because we don't know their real definition, but because there is no real "definition" to them. To suppose that there *must* be would be like supposing that whenever children play with a ball they play a game according to strict rules' (BB, p. 25).

224 We are always looking for an exact form of usage, because we orient ourselves according to the natural sciences and mathematics. When we philosophize we are not supposed to compare our use of words with something which is accomplished according to exact rules. Precisely from this attitude towards language arise the puzzles which we are trying to clear out of the way. 'Consider as an example the question "What is time?" as Saint Augustine and others have asked it. At first sight what this question asks for is a definition, but then immediately the question arises: "What should we gain by a definition, as it can only lead us to other undefined term?" And why should one be puzzled just by the lack of a definition of time, and not by the lack of a definition of "chair"? Why shouldn't we be puzzled in all cases where we haven't got a definition?' (BB, p. 26.) We falsely assume that a definition will free us from embarrassment. If we then answer with a definition, and immediately discover nevertheless that it is false, we would have to replace it by another definition, the correct one, and so on.

225 A word does not have a meaning which as it were was given to it by a power independent of us, so that one could undertake a scientific investigation about what the word *really*

means. Rather, *someone* gave the words their meanings. And because meanings have been given there are words with several clearly circumscribed meanings. But most words are used in a thousand different ways which little by little fuse into one another. It is therefore not possible to set up strict rules for their use or to give definitions.

226 That is also true for the language of philosophy. In philosophy we are in no way dealing with an ideal language in contrast to our everyday language. That is, we cannot at all improve our everyday language. It is completely in order. If we construct 'ideal languages' then our goal is mainly this: that we want to eliminate someone's embarrassment, which has arisen through his believing that he understood the precise use of a word of everyday language and then used it one-sidedly and falsely (see BB, p. 28). The task of philosophy is to liberate authentic understanding by eliminating misunderstandings. 'The task of philosophy is not to create a new, ideal language, but to clarify the linguistic usage of our language – the one which exists. Its goal is to eliminate specific misunderstandings; not, as it were, to first create an authentic understanding' (PG 72).

That a word has no strict meaning is, therefore, just as little a failing as the assumption that the light of my reading lamp is not a real light because it does not have a sharp boundary (see BB, p. 27).

227 What we have to understand by precision depends on the goal we put to ourselves. We can simply not define an ideal of precision. It is unnecessary and for the most part even unusable. We attain our goal better with something that in opposition to an apparent ideal of exactness is criticized as 'inexact'.

'If I tell someone: "stand roughly here" – may not this explanation work perfectly? And cannot every other one fail too?

'But isn't it an inexact explanation? – Yes; why shouldn't we call it "inexact"? Only let us understand what "inexact" means. For it does not mean "unusable". And let us consider what we call "exact" explanation in contrast with this one. Perhaps something like drawing a chalk line round an area? Here it strikes us at once that the line has breadth. So a colour-edge would be more exact. But has this exactness still got a function here: isn't the engine idling? And remember too that we have not yet defined what is to count as overstepping this exact boundary; how, with what instruments, it is to be established. And so on.

'We understand what it means to set a pocket-watch to the exact time or to regulate it to be exact. But what if it were asked: is this exactness an ideal exactness, or how nearly does it approach the ideal? – Of course, we can speak of measurements of time in which there is a different, and as we should say a greater, exactness than in the measurement of time by a pocket-watch; in which the words "to set the clock to the exact time" have a different, though related meaning, and "to tell the time" is a different process and so on. – Now, if I tell someone: "You should come to dinner more punctually; you know it begins at one o'clock exactly" – is there really no question of *exactness* here? because it is possible to say: "Think of the determination of time in the laboratory or the observatory; *there* you see what 'exactness' means"?'

' "Inexact" is really a reproach, and "exact" is praise. And that is to say that what is inexact attains its goal less perfectly than what is more exact. Thus the point here is what we call "the goal". Am I inexact when I do not give our distance from the sun to the nearest foot, or tell a joiner the width of a table to the nearest thousandth of an inch?

'No *single* ideal of exactness has been laid down; we do not know what we should be supposed to imagine under this head – unless you yourself lay down what is to be so called. But you will find it difficult to hit upon such a convention; at least any that satisfies you' (PI 88).

An ideal exactness would not make the concept more usable in any case. If I say: 'The ground is completely covered with plants', it is then nonsensical to give a precise account of the ground or to define exactly the concept of a plant. It contributes nothing to the exactness of my statement, which is completely useful as it is and therefore does not need to become more usable (see PI 70).

Often what is not distinct is exactly what we need and not something allegedly distinct. For example, a picture that is not distinct can let us get to know another person better than a sharply engraved one. What is genuinely useful, then, is what is not distinct. '"But is a blurred concept a concept at all?" – Is an indistinct photograph a picture of a person at all? Is it even always an advantage to replace an indistinct picture by a sharp one? Isn't the indistinct one often exactly what we need?' (PI 71.)

228 In order to use a word appropriately we do not need to give an explanation for it. We can, therefore, use a concept without having to be able to also describe its application. Should we still want to try such a description, it would be possible that it would be totally inadequate. 'Just like the majority of people if they would want to try to describe correctly the use of money' (z 525). It is just like the case of my room, of which I have an impression as a whole and in which is assembled everything which I normally find in it. 'One could say: I would have no impression of the room as a whole if I could not let my gaze roam about quickly here and there and if I could not let myself move around freely in it. (Stream of thought.) But now the question is, how is the fact that I "have an impression of it as a whole" manifested? For example, in the matter-of-fact way in which I find my way about in it; in the absence of looking about, of doubting, of amazement. In the fact that enumerable activities are limited by its walls and that I put all that together in my discourse as "my room". In the fact that I find it useful and necessary to avail myself again and again of the concept of "my room" in contrast to its walls, corners, etc.' (z 203).

II

229 There is another kind of vagueness other than that of the indefiniteness of meaning, which nevertheless is related to it, namely, imprecision in terms of exact measurement. 'As soon as one wants to apply exact concepts of measurement to immediate experience, one runs up against a distinctive vagueness in this experience. That is, however, only a vagueness relative to those measurement concepts. And it now seems to me that this blurredness is not something preliminary that more precise knowledge will later eliminate, but a characteristic logical peculiarity.

If I say, for example: "I now see a red circle on a blue ground and remember that I saw one a few minutes ago which was identically large or perhaps somewhat smaller and a little lighter", *this* experience is not to be described more exactly' (PR 211).

230   This whole problematic becomes clear through the problem: how many grains of sand make a heap? I can say, for example: a group of more than one hundred grains is a heap, and a group of less than ten is not a heap. The delimitation is then, first, arbitrary and, secondly, not exact, for one hundred or ten are not limits which are essential to the heap. One is dealing here with constantly provisional highest and lowest boundaries. And the order: 'Make me the smallest heap which you still call a heap!' I could not comply with (see PG, p. 240). This shows that also an exact delimitation of inexactness is impossible. 'Just as if one marked off a bog by a wall, the wall is not, however, *the* boundary of the bog, but it only encircles it on solid ground. It is a sign that there is a bog inside it, but not that the bog is just as large as the surface enclosed by it' (PR 211).

231   Another example of inherent vagueness lies in the description of an object in the distance. The description will not, that is, become more precise through my saying what I notice about it by going closer to it and taking a look, for then it is no longer the object in the distance (see PI 171). It does not become more precise by a closer look.

To draw a sharp boundary often makes just as little sense as taking a 'closer' look. What would we do if we were supposed to oppose to a vague image a 'corresponding' clear one? That would be a hopeless task, for just when the image became sharp it could not correspond to the vague one (see PI 77).

232   The word 'precision' is related in everyday language to a comparison. Where, therefore, a certain degree of imprecision is present there must also be present greater and ultimately complete precision.

If I say: 'I never see a precise circle' or: 'I never see a sharp line', then there has to be a precise circle or a sharp line. But an exact circle in the visual field is unthinkable (see PR 213). The exact circle is not something which I see but it is an infinite possibility of increasing the precision itself which I call the circle (see PR 215).

The problem arises through our using two languages: a language of visual space and a language of Euclidean space (see W, p. 59). If one wants to apply the concepts of one to the other in this way there immediately arises a specific vagueness (see PR 211).

Visual space and Euclidean space follow different rules. Let us imagine a line composed of twenty-four sections and a second, beside the first, composed of twenty-five equally large sections. In visual space the two lines appear equally long. And that does not mean that in visual space something appears other than it is. The difference between the two segments is not given in visual space (see PR 208, 209).

Precisely because certain distinctions are not given in visual space, the inferential methods of Euclidean space can lead to baffling results if we apply them to visual space. The elements of visual space are not joined together in a visual whole, which we would have foreseen, but in another construction. For example, we can indeed see a small section taken from a large circle as a straight line. But if we proceed in this way we are not investigating visual space as visual space, but Euclidean space is constantly intruding upon it. 'It is a matter of explaining certain contradictions if we apply to visual space the inferential methods of Euclidean space.

'I mean: it is possible to pursue in visual space a construction (therefore, an inferential chain) all of whose steps we understand, but whose result contradicts our geometrical concepts.

'Now I believe that that results from our being able to see the construction only stepwise but not as a unity. This explanation would be, therefore, that there is no such thing as a visual construction which would be composed of these individual visual pieces. That would be as if I showed someone a small segment of a large round surface and asked him whether he recognized the largest circle visible on it as a straight line; and if he had done that, I should turn the ball and would show him that he would come back again to the same place on the circle.

L

I still did not prove to him in this way that something like a straight line in visual space doubles back on itself.

'This explanation would, therefore, be: those are visible *pieces* which are not assembled into a visual whole or in any case not to a whole whose final result I believe I see at the end.

'The simplest construction of this sort would be, then, the one above of the two equally long segments in which one proceeds to derive one piece n-times and in the other $n+1$ times. The steps of the construction would be a proceeding from one part to another and the establishing of the equality of these pieces.

'Here it would be possible to explain that by proceeding in this way I do not really investigate the original visual image with the equally long segments. But something else intrudes into the investigation, which then leads to the baffling result' (PR 210).

233 Not only can we use vague and undefined concepts correctly, but of course we can also use them falsely. They show their genuine usefulness and therefore their appropriateness which, as we saw, has nothing to do with indefiniteness inherent in them, when we apply them simultaneously to their antithesis. If, for example, in everyday speech usage the opposite of 'indefinite' is 'clear', we can see that the indefiniteness of meanings can not at all be measured by an ideal of clarity. Just as the opposition of inexact and exact showed us that it is not possible to define an ideal of precision. How we are able to use our words is shown in praxis. They must fit. If we use a word with reference to its antithesis, then we do not thereby eliminate its apparent indefiniteness, we remove the possibility of a confusion. 'As in this example the word "solidity" was used wrongly and it seemed that we had shown that nothing really was solid, just in this way, in stating our puzzles about the flux of all phenomena, we are using the words "flux" and "vagueness" wrongly, in a typical metaphysical way, namely without an antithesis; whereas in their correct and every-day use vagueness is opposed to clearness, flux to stability, inaccuracy to accuracy, and *problem* to solution' (BB, pp. 45–6).

L

GRAMMAR AND LOGIC

I

234   Grammar investigates the relations between language and reality. Grammar is the totality of rules which state in which connections words have meaning and propositions make sense (see w, p. 220). It describes in such a way that it delimits what is describable. It describes the use of words in language and the conditions for the representation of reality through propositions (see PG 23, 345). The experiences which we need in both cases for the construction of a grammar are different. 'There are two completely different concepts of "experience". Experience which we need to determine the truth of an assertion is a completely different experience than that which we need for understanding a word. Only an experience of the first kind is expressed in propositions' (w, p. 217).

Philosophy is the clarification of grammar and it is thereby the grasping of the essence of the world. We see that language cannot express what belongs to the essence of the world. But in so far as philosophy states the rules for how what is non-sensical is excluded it allows us to grasp the essence of the world. 'For what belongs to the essence of the world just cannot be *said*. And philosophy, if it could say something, would have to describe the essence of the world.

'The essence of language is, however, a picture of the essence of the world, and philosophy as custodian of grammar can in fact grasp the essence of the world only not in the propositions of language but in rules for this language which exclude non-sensical combinations of signs' (PR 54).

235   Grammar is not concerned with the question whether this experimental proposition is true and that one is false. It asks

rather what are the conditions and what is the method of the comparison with reality. This comparison is, however, not like the comparison of a picture with the reality being pictured, but it shows what and how the proposition (the picture) represents or can represent. The comparison of the proposition with reality is, therefore, nothing less than the showing of the conditions of its understanding, of its sense (see PG 45).

'The rules of grammar are not justified by one's showing that their use leads to the representation's agreeing with reality. For this justification would have to describe what is being represented itself' (PG 134). Reality first becomes something represented in the process of representation. The fundamental question is, therefore: how do I represent anything? This is, again, a grammatical determination. We can also say: 'grammar tells us what kind of thing an object is' (PI 373).

236　The connection – and hence the comparison – between language and reality is effected by the clarification of words and meanings. As these belong to grammar, language remains closed in itself, autonomous (see PG 55). The harmony between thought and reality is to be discovered in the grammar of language. 'If you ask me: where do I know that from? I answer simply: from the fact that I understand the meaning of the utterance' (w, p. 78). If I say: 'This combination of words makes no sense', I exclude it in this way from the domain of language and hence from the world. With that I run up against the limit of language and the limit of the world (see PI 499).

II

237　Grammar does not say how language *has* to be constructed; it investigates and describes the use of language. It describes but it does not explain (see PI 496). If, for example, I determine that the meaning of a word lies not in its purpose or its effect, but in its use, in its application, then this results from a grammatical investigation.

In grammar we ask: what is deposited in the sign? How is the word or the sign used? What do we do with it? The connection in which a sign is joined with reality *is* already to some extent reality, is always a connection in grammar. For whence do I know that this picture of . . . is a picture of . . . ? I *apply* it in this way (see RFM I-128, 129). Or, for example, if I understand by 'space' Euclidean space, then geometry is the grammar of the words with which I describe the phenomena of this space. 'The geometry being used is the grammar of the statements about the spatial objects' (PG, p. 319). Geometry stands in the relation of possibility to reality. If I understand by 'space' physical space, then geometry is no longer a grammar. It is then not related to what I see but is related to the experiences of measuring and is then just like physics, an hypothesis (see W, p. 162).

'One could almost speak of an external and an internal geometry. What is arrayed in visual space stands in this *kind* of order *a priori*, that is, according to its logical nature, and here geometry is simply grammar. What the physicist puts into relation with one another in the geometry of physical space are instrument readings, which according to their *inner* nature are not different whether we live in a linear or a spherical space. That is, it is not the investigation of the logical properties of these readings which leads the physicist to his assumption about the kind of physical space, but the facts which have been derived from these readings.

'The geometry of physics in this sense has to do not with possibility but with facts. It is confirmed by facts; in the sense, that is, in which a *part* of an hypothesis is confirmed' (PR 178).

238   If I conduct business, then I conduct negotiations, talk to my partners on the telephone, invite them to dinner. But what is business itself? It is the transaction which is recorded in my ledgers. 'Grammar – those are the ledgers of language out of which everything which does not concern accompanying sensations but the factual transactions of language has to be derived' (PG 44).

239   If, for example, I want to investigate the transactions which lie behind the word 'know', if, therefore, I carry out a grammatical investigation, then I discover that 'knowing' has something to do with 'discover'. That is to say, I discover that by asking: just what does 'knowing' signify? What criteria do I

use for its employment? 'We said that it was a way of examining grammar (the use) of the word "know", to ask ourselves
what, in the particular case we are examining, we should call
"getting to know". There is a temptation to think that this
question is only vaguely relevant, if relevant at all, to the
question: "what is the meaning of the word 'to know'?" We
seem to be on a side-track when we ask the question: "What is
it like in this case 'to get to know'?" But this question is really
a question concerning the grammar of the word "to know",
and this becomes clearer if we put it in the form: "What do we
call 'getting to know'?" It is part of the grammar of the word
"chair" that *this* is what we call "to sit on a chair", and it is
part of the grammar of the word "meaning" that *this* is what
we call "explanation of meaning"; in the same way to explain
my criterion for another person's having toothache is to give a
grammatical explanation about the word "toothache" and in
this sense, an explanation concerning the meaning of the word
"toothache" ' (BB, pp. 23–4).

240   In grammatical investigations the question of criteria is
always a very important one.

To be sure, it is for the most part such a question that drives
us from grammar in the usual sense to philosophical grammar.
What is related to grammar in the normal sense we want to call
'grammatical". We find an example for the importance of
criteria in states. 'Expectation is, grammatically, a state: as: to
be of an opinion, to hope something, to know something, to be
able to do something. But to understand the grammar of these
states one has to ask: "What counts as a criterion for anyone's
being in such a state?" (States of hardness, of weight, of fitting)'
(PI 572).

To avoid specific confusions we can also introduce besides the
concept of the criterion the opposing concept of the symptom.
To the question: 'Whence do you know that such and such is
the case?' we answer sometimes by giving criteria and sometimes by giving symptoms. 'I call "symptom" a phenomenon
of which experience has taught us that it coincided, in some way

or other, with the phenomenon which is our defining criterion' (BB, p. 25). In praxis for the most part the distinction between what phenomenon is a criterion and what a symptom is obliterated. Nevertheless the antithetical pair can sometimes help us to discover what grammar is being used.

241 In grammar nothing 'new' is uncovered. We can only uncover and express clearly what we have always already unconsciously done. When once the word giving the solution is found there is nevertheless no surprise. We have the feeling: you knew that for a long time already! The results of philosophy appear, therefore, in a certain way always trivial (see w, p. 77).

242 What our grammar lacks above all is clarity (*Übersichtlichkeit*) (see PR 1). One has to try to formulate everything in the clearest way possible. As long as there are different opinions about a thesis that is a sign that one has not expressed himself clearly enough. In the case of a full and clear formulation there are no longer any hesitations and oppositions. 'If, however, one gets clear about the grammar by proceeding in completely small steps, whereby every single step becomes completely evident, in this way, in general, no discussion can arise' (w, p. 183).

243 If we want to undertake such a step-wise presentation of a grammatical investigation, we can determine that dissatisfaction with the grammar being used is often directed against the use of a definite expression in connection with definite criteria. We have to create clarity about this, then, and show, especially, that the uneasiness accordingly derives from our being tempted alternatively to use a word in several different meanings.

'And it is particularly difficult to discover that an assertion which the metaphysician makes expresses discontentment with our grammar when the words of this assertion can also be used to state a fact of experience. Thus when he says: "only my pain is real pain", this sentence might mean that the other people are only pretending. And when he says: "this tree doesn't exist when nobody sees it", this might mean: "this tree vanishes when we turn our backs to it". The man who says: "only my pain is real", doesn't mean to say that he has found out by the common criteria – the criteria, i.e., which give our words their common meanings – that the others who said they had pains were cheating. But what he rebels against is the use of *this* expression in connection with *these* criteria. That is, he objects to using this word in the particular way in which it is commonly used. On the other hand, he is not aware that he is objecting to a convention. He sees a way of dividing the country different from the one used on the ordinary map. He feels tempted, say, to say the name "Devonshire" not for the county with its conventional boundary, but for a region differently bounded. He could express this by saying: "Isn't it absurd to make *this* a county, to draw the boundaries *here*?" But what he says is: 'The *real* Devonshire is this." We could answer: 'But what you want is only a new notation, and by a new notation no facts of geography are changed." It is true, however, that we may be irresistibly attracted or repelled by a notation. (We easily forget how much a notation, a form of expression, may mean to us, and that changing it isn't always as easy as it often is in mathematics or in the sciences. A change of clothes or of names may mean very little and it may mean a great deal.)

'I shall try to elucidate the problem discussed by realists, idealists, and solipsists by showing you a problem closely related to it. It is this: "Can we have unconscious thoughts, unconscious feelings, etc.?" The idea of there being unconscious thoughts has revolted many people. Others again have said that these were wrong in supposing that there could only be conscious thoughts, and that psychoanalysis had discovered unconscious ones. The objectors to unconscious thought did not see that they were not objecting to the newly discovered psychological reactions; that they had done more than discover new psychological reactions; that they had, in a sense, discovered conscious thoughts which were unconscious. The first could have stated their objection by saying: "We don't wish to use the phrase 'unconscious thoughts'; we wish to reserve the word 'thought' for what you call 'conscious thoughts'." They state their case wrongly when they say: "There can only be conscious thoughts and no unconscious ones." For if they don't wish to talk of "unconscious thoughts" they should not use the phrase "conscious thought" either' (BB, pp. 56–8).

We ourselves are often blind to the fact that we have strong prejudices for or against certain forms of expression (see z 323).

We have to try, therefore, to find a presentation which satisfies our needs for clarity and eliminates our uneasiness. In this way it can simply happen that we have to emphasize differences more strongly than everyday language does. Or that we employ forms of expression which have more of a resemblance with one another and accordingly signify more resemblance than in our everyday language.

IV

244   We are also led, finally, to have to distinguish between a 'surface grammar' and a 'depth grammar'. 'In the use of words one might distinguish "surface grammar" from "depth grammar". What immediately impresses itself upon us about the use of a word is the way it is used in the construction of the sentence, the part of its use – one might say – that can be taken in by the ear. – And now compare the depth grammar, say of the word "to mean", with what its surface grammar would lead us to suspect. No wonder we find it difficult to know our way about' (PI 644).

V

245   The foundation of grammar is the distinction between sense and non-sense. 'I would like to say: "I have to *begin* with the distinction between sense and non-sense. Before that nothing is possible. I cannot justify it"' (PG 81). Having presupposed this foundation, grammar consists of combinations (see PG 138).

246   It completely depends upon our grammar what we call possible and what, not. We are accordingly inclined to call grammar arbitrary (see PG 82). 'Grammar is not accountable to reality. Grammatical rules first determine the meaning (they constitute it) and are therefore responsible to no meaning and are to this extent arbitrary.

'There can be no discussion about whether these rules or others are the right ones for the word "not" (that is, whether they are in conformity with its meaning). For the word without these rules still has no meaning and if we change the rules it now has another meaning (or none) and we can then just as well also change the word (. . .). Why do I not call the rules of cooking arbitrary; and why am I tempted to call arbitrary the rules of grammar? Because I consider the concept "cooking" as defined by the goal of cooking, but not, on the contrary, the concept "language" by the goal of language. He who directs himself in cooking by other rules than the correct ones cooks badly; but (. . .) the person who directs himself by other grammatical rules than, say, the normal ones, does not therefore say something false, but speaks about something else' (PG 133).

247   But *reality* is not arbitrary. If things were other than they in fact are, then our normal language-games would lose their point. 'The procedure of putting a lump of cheese on a balance and fixing the price by the turn of the scale would lose its point if it frequently happened for such lumps to suddenly grow or shrink for no obvious reason' (PI 142).

248   We have to be in agreement with reality. 'If there did not exist any agreement in what we call "red", etc., etc., then language would cease' (RFM II-70; see Z 430, 351). Men agree with one another in respect to certain things, namely by using words as language (see RFM I-152). Outside of language there is no agreement. And without agreement there is no language.

249   And we have to stick to the rules which have once been established. 'Indeed, but is a rule not something arbitrary? Something that I *establish*? And could I establish that the multiplication 18×15 is *not* supposed to give 270? – Why not? – But then it has just not happened according to the rule which I first set up and whose use I have practised' (RFM V-31).

We have to be able to come to agreement about a difference in the result of a calculation. But that means that we arrive at an identical calculation. One person cannot perform a calculation with another result than another. One of them then just does not perform a calculation (see RFM V-6).

'How, then, does one begin to establish that a formula is false? For example, the formula $7 \times 5 = 30$? How do I know that if $7 \times 5 = 35$, it is not also 31? What would we then do if someone says: '8×7=75'"? We would say: "Well now, what are you up to? That is just false"! If he now were to answer us: "Well, how so? I have just established it this way", we could only say to him: "Well, then you are just using another calculus than the usual one which is called multiplication. We do not know your calculus. If we proceed according to the rules which are given to us, then 8×7=56 and not 75, and that is the contradiction."

'If someone says that 8×7=75 then he is correct in that regard just as much or just as little as if he were to define the word "table" in a completely new way. The definition is certainly arbitrary. But in spite of this one can say that a definition is false if it does not in fact contradict what one actually means. In this sense also the formula 8×7=75 is false' (w, pp. 177f).

250   The relation between arbitrariness and non-arbitrariness in grammar is simply already given by the fact that a proposition, in order to be true or false, therefore in order to be able to be in agreement with reality, has to distinguish itself from reality (see w, p. 239). It represents reality, but it is not reality itself. It also does not represent all of reality. The proposition can represent in this way or another. Even if the proposition is true, a certain arbitrariness is found in the method of its mode of representation (see PG 82).

The relation of arbitrariness and non-arbitrariness in grammar consists further in its rules being projected in the closest connection with reality, but not resulting from it by inner necessity. 'The rules of grammar are arbitrary in the same sense as the choice of a unit of measure' (PG 133). But that can only mean that the unit of measure is dependent upon the length of an object that I want to measure, that is, that there is not a 'true' and a 'false' unit of measure, that I, however, have to choose a unit of measure if I want to measure and that I am restricted within it (see PG 140). A map's method of projection is arbitrary; but the map is true if it represents reality (see PG 51).

251   Our grammar, that is, our conceptual formation, which directs our experience in certain channels, is often such that

only through it do we see a definite kind of fact (see RFM III-33, 48, V-15; z 357, 358).

252   Grammar does not address itself to empirical universality but to a universality of the ultimate rules of the game whose validity is beyond appeal (see PG, p. 215).

VI

253   What counts as an adequate proof of a statement belongs to logic (see OC 82). But logic is not an empirical science, for its propositions are not to be tested by experience; they are rules of testing (see OC 98). 'But does one then have to say that there are no sharp boundaries between propositions of logic and experimental propositions? The lack of sharpness is just that of a boundary between *rule* and experiential proposition (OC 319).

254   That a proposition is true or false really only means that a decision for or against it is possible. What does the reason for such a decision look like? How can an experiential proposition be tested, what counts as a test, what is tested by it, who makes the decision, what determines what the reason is (PG 109, 110, 125, 200)?

It is experience itself which teaches us to judge in such a way that it is correct to judge in this way. 'If it is the *reason* that we judge in this way (and not just the cause), we do not again have a reason to consider this as a reason' (OC 130). The whole problem, however, is how experience teaches us the verification of itself, how it shows itself as a reason. 'Do I not more and more come to say that, in the last analysis, logic cannot be described? You have to consider the praxis of language, then you will see it' (PG 501). Logic is not a kind of super-physics, a description of the logical structure of the world which we would perceive through a kind of super-experience (see RFM I-8).

So-called logical propositions *show* the logical properties of language and therefore of the universe, but *say* nothing (cf. T 6.12).

'This means that by merely looking at them you can *see* these properties. whereas, in a proposition proper, you cannot see what is true by looking at it (cf. т 6.113).

'It is impossible to *say* what these properties are, because in order to do so, you would need a language, which hadn't got the properties in question, and it is impossible that this should be a *proper* language. Impossible to construct an illogical language.

'In order that you should have a language which can express or *say* everything that *can* be said, this language must have certain properties; and when this is the case, *that* it has them can no longer be said in that language or *any* language.

'An illogical language would be one in which, e.g., you could put an *event* into a hole.

'Thus a language which *can* express everything *mirrors* certain properties of the world by these properties which it must have; and logical so-called propositions show *in a systematic way* those properties' (NB, p. 107).

'Logic is not a body of doctrine, but a mirror-image of the world' (т 6.13).

M

GIVENNESS

I

255   We have already seen that agreement, if it were complete, would not exist at all; its concept would then be totally unknown. We are rooted in reality and remain so, we reduplicate it in a certain way by representing it. Its connection with reality and the possibility of its being in agreement with it lie in the kind and manner of representation. That it is true that we always start out from reality is shown in 'knowing that one can show if . . ., that one, therefore, can recognize it if one sees it' (see PI 388; PR 11).

256   This knowing which can always eventuate in a seeing is really no duplication of seeing, but rather 'a knowing in and through the very act of seeing' (*Sehen im Sehen*). ' "Verifying by inspection" is a totally misleading expression. That is, it says that first there occurs an event, the inspection, and that this would be comparable to looking through a microscope or to the event of turning one's head *in order to see something*. And that then seeing *has* to succeed. One could speak of "seeing by turning around" or "seeing by taking a look". But then even the turning around (or gazing) is an event external to seeing, which accordingly only has a practical interest for us. What one would like to say is: "Seeing by seeing" ' (z 436).

257   The problem is to stop with what really happens and what is shown in 'seeing in seeing', in 'seeing by seeing'. If everything is described when we 'see' the agreement, we would often still like to look ever further. The problem is that for the most part we do not at all see an ultimate description as the solution to a

question which we had posed. By looking for a further explanation we overlook the reason that what is – how it is – and what
occurs – how it occurs – shows itself. The proto-phenomenon is
just what is described and not something that would still lie
behind it.

'Here we run up against a marvellous and characteristic
phenomenon in philosophical investigations: the difficulty –
I could say – is not to find the solution but to recognize as the
solution something which looks as if it were only a preliminary
step to it. "We have already said everything. – Not something
which follows from that but just *that* is the solution"! That
hangs together, I believe, with our falsely expecting an explanation; while a description is the solution of the difficulty; *if* we
fit it correctly into our treatment. If we stay with it, and do not
try to proceed beyond it.

'The difficulty is here: to call a halt' (z 314).

In this context it is to be noted that the most important
aspects of things for us are hidden by their simplicity and
everyday character. That they lie constantly before our eyes
hinders, to some degree, their being noticed, or rather hinders
us from noticing how important they are (see PI 415). What does
not catch our attention does not make an *impression* of not
doing so, but rather: it just does not catch our attention (see
PI 600). 'The real foundations of his inquiry do not strike a man
at all. Unless *that* fact has at some time struck him. – And this
means: we fail to be struck by what, once seen, is most striking
and powerful' (PI 129). The perspective is, therefore, turned
around. What is the most striking and important for the philosopher is normally overlooked.

If after a description which is a solution one still looks for an
explanation, one would get no further and would only again be
led back to the description (see z 315). 'He who finds the road
sign does not look for further instruction, but rather he simply
goes' (z 277).

II

258 The phenomenon is what happens, it is perceived by
us (see PG 97). It is given. If I cannot appeal to anything else

for the verification of a proposition, then I have arrived at an originary-givenness, then I have to call a halt and accept it. There is then no 'then', but rather the origin of the 'then'.

'I can indeed say: "This conductor is electrically charged; *for* the electroscope shows a deflection." But I cannot say: "The spot in the visual field is yellow; *for* . . ." ' (w, p. 249). If I see yellow and recognize yellow, then 'I cannot any longer look for a *sign* that this is yellow, but this is the fact itself; I have penetrated up to the last point, beyond which it is not possible to go. Regarding the immediately given I may not form any *hypotheses*' (w, p. 97).

That is also as if someone asked me: 'What is the difference between blue and red?' Then I answer: 'The one is red and the other is blue' (see PG, p. 208). ' "It seems red to me." – "And how is red?" "Like this" ' (z 420).

259 It is so difficult to begin with something – or to return to the beginning – which for us is the beginning. We would like most of all to place ourselves outside the world and to see where and how it begins. To begin before the beginning, to go behind the beginning. Not even the attempt to articulate this can happen. It can only be represented in an inarticulate cry, and with that eliminate itself.

'It is so difficult to find the *beginning*. Or better: it is difficult to begin at the beginning. And not to try to go further behind it' (OC 471). If I have arrived at an immediately given I cannot proceed further behind it. What was supposed to be still more immediate would cease to be a description of the given. I cannot penetrate to what is before the given, to what, so to speak, brings forth the given. 'There would come out, then, instead of a description, that inarticulate sound with which many authors would like so much to begin philosophy. "(I have consciousness of something by knowing my knowing.") It is just not possible to begin before the beginning' (PR 68).

III

260 Description points to what is immediately given, it allows us to grasp it, but it is not itself what is given. If I gaze at the

blue sky and say: 'How blue the sky is!' then I point neither towards myself, towards, therefore, the fact that I experience the sky as blue, nor do I advert to the words with which I say this, but rather: I *see* the blue.

In a certain way the description of the immediately given is no description at all, for the words do not *contain* it, they show it. 'Describe the aroma of coffee. – Why can't it be done? Do we lack the words? And *for what* are words lacking? – But how do we get the idea that such a description must after all be possible? Have you ever felt the lack of such a description? Have you tried to describe the aroma and not succeeded?

'((I should like to say: "These notes say something glorious, but I do not know what." "These notes are a powerful gesture, but I cannot put anything side by side with it that will serve as an explanation." A grave nod. James: "Our vocabulary is inadequate." Then why don't we introduce a new one? What would have to be the case for us to be able to?))' (PI 610.)

What is immediately given is beyond language. 'The aroma is glorious!' There is no doubt about that. And yet I cannot catch the aroma itself in words (see z 551; LAC, p. 11; w, p. 236).

261   We said that the immediately given of experience is beyond language. That is no failing but rather shows the possibility of description itself. The description of the world through propositions is, that is, only possible if what is being signified is not its own sign but rather if it is to some extent duplicated by signs which stand for it. Only because the representation is different from what is represented is it possible for it to be true or false (see w, p. 239; NB, p. 15).

The possibility of a proposition, of a description, is based therefore on objects being represented by signs – but not being contained in this representation – and that the given is not its own sign.

'Objects can only be *named*. Signs are their representatives. I can only speak *about* them: I cannot *put them into words*. Propositions can only say *how* things are; not *what* they are' (T 3.221).

262   The face of others is also given to me immediately: their facial expression, their suffering, their anger, their mood, their

friendliness, their gaze. 'We do not look upon the human eye as a receiver (. . .). The ear receives; the eye looks. (It casts glances, it gazes, beams, lights up.) It is possible to still fear with the eye, not with the ear or the nose. If you look at the eye you see something go out from it. You see the glance of the eye' (z 222).

But how does one see emotions? As opposed to what? I see the face immediately, in its emotion, and describe it as radiant with happiness, bored, sad, and so on. We do not associate the one or the other feeling with the face; they are given immediately, personified in the face; the feeling *has* the facial characteristics (see z 225; PG 128; PI 537). But how am I now to describe joy, sadness, boredom, and so on? Are they not, once again, something immediate? And do I have to describe them at all; can I even do so? Are not goodness, cowardice, mildness first and foremost given in the face itself? 'If I were asked whether I could imagine a chair with a friendly expression, I would want to imagine it certainly above all with a friendly *facial expression*. I would want to read into it a friendly *face*' (PG 129).

IV

263   Immediate experience is the end. 'A proposition, an hypothesis, is coupled with reality in a more or less loose fashion. In the limit case there is no longer any connection; reality can do what it wants without coming into conflict with the proposition; then the proposition, the hypothesis, is senseless. All that is essential is that the signs refer, in no matter how complicated a way, at the end to immediate experience and not to an intermediate link (a thing in itself)' (PR 225).

One does not get past immediate experience as an end of justification, because one does not get free of experience at all, because it is not possible to go beyond experience. 'It is possible only to seem "to go beyond every possible experience"; indeed, this word only seemingly makes sense because it is formed by analogy to meaningful expressions' (z 260). 'Those philosophers who think that it is possible to extend, as it were, experience by thinking should heed that it is possible to transmit speech over the telephone but not the measles' (PR 66).

264   Immediate experience, which has its meaning in itself, is to be accepted. It is a form of life. Even if we determine reality, even if we, in common actions, create something new, the fact that we do this or can do this is to be understood as a given form of life, and only as such. 'What is to be accepted, the given are – one could say – *forms of life*' (PI, p. 226). 'It is only possible here to *describe* and to say: such is human life' (BGB, p. 236). The fabric of life is composed of forms of life and their modifications together (see PI, p. 174).

265   Perhaps the originary givens, as given to me in primary forms of life, are colours, space, time, the faces of others, their ways of acting, and other such givens (see PR 147).

V

266   What is given, what is to be accepted, *leads* us. 'Let us study the use of the expression "to be guided" by studying the use of the word "reading"' (BB, p. 119). First of all, we can say, in general and quite universally, that we *read* reality, we read the world. Secondly, the given leads us when we reduplicate it with itself and represent it in language. We can better understand this leading by what is given in the reduplication of itself if we take a look at what occurs in the case of following something already really reduplicated, namely, the reading of something written.

267   What is going on when we read (see BB, pp. 119f)? Let us try this explanation: someone reads when he derives the reproduction from the original (see PI 162). But then we see that that is only a special case. We use the word 'reading' for a family of cases. I could also say that what is written enters into the sound of what is spoken, that a unity, an alloy is formed; that in the process of reading I see *and* hear. Still, when I read I take no notice of that (see PI 171).

What is genuine and characteristic about reading consists, however, in the following: the words *come* in a specific way. They do not come the way they would if, for example, I were to invent them. They come *of themselves* (see PI 165, 166). The reading glance, that is, the comprehending look, is led in such a way that it glides along, but it does not slip (see PI 168).

But in reading do we not experience a kind of causing of our understanding by the given word images (see PI 169)? Certainly, I am led in a certain way. 'I should like to say: "Sure enough, I was guided there. But as for what is characteristic in what happened – If I say what happened, I no longer find it characteristic."

'But now notice this: *while* I am being guided everything is quite simple, I notice nothing *special*; but afterwards, when I ask myself what it was that happened, it seems to have been something indescribable. *Afterwards* no description satisfies me' (PI 175). I remember, that is, nothing and still it seems as if something else had to have happened: for was I not really led, was there no influence? 'When I look back on the experience I have the feeling that what is essential about it is an "experience of being influenced", of a connection – as opposed to any mere simultaneity of phenomena: but at the same time I should not be willing to call any experienced phenomenon the "experience of being influenced". . . . I should like to say that I had experienced the *"because"*, and yet I do not want to call any phenomenon the "experience of the cause"' (PI 176). We experience 'being guided' and 'because' without having an experience of being guided or because (see *Eine Philosophische Betrachtung, Schriften,* 5, pp. 183ff).

VI

268 A proposition, language, describes and says reality. Reality is shown in the describing language, it is represented; but reality is not the representation, language *is* not reality. Reality is said in language, yet saying is no hauling in of something.

If we now come to the saying of saying itself, we have to determine that this saying is not able to be said. 'How can it be *communicated* to me *how* the proposition represents? Or can that simply not be *said* to me? And if that is true, can I *"know"* it? If it were supposed to be said to me this would have to happen by means of a proposition: but that could only show it.

'What can be said can be said by a proposition. Therefore, nothing that is necessary for the understanding of *all* propositions can be said' (NB, p. 25).

If we can only be conscious of the saying of saying, if we can only show it, we also have, conversely, to determine that what we can show cannot be said (see T 4.1212). 'What is mirrored in language I cannot express by means of it' (NB, p. 132).

269   If a proposition is supposed to be able to say reality, if a proposition makes sense and is supposed to be able to be true or false, that is, if it is supposed to be able to be in agreement with reality, then in the proposition itself there has to be something identical with reality (see NB, p. 15). The proposition cannot represent what it has to have in common with reality in order to be able to represent it, for then it would have to step outside of itself and of reality (see T 4.12).

What the proposition has in common with reality and what it itself can no longer represent we call its (logical) form. That it can represent reality is always already presupposed in its form. (This 'form' has, note well, nothing to do with the 'packaging' proper to logical formalization.) 'Propositions cannot represent the logical form; it is mirrored in them' (T 4.121).

The form is not describable, not utterable, for it is represented only *in* describing, *in* saying. A meaning can be investigated, a concept can be explained, a form has to show itself (see W, p. 220).

270   We are led very quickly to the – indefinable – form if we want to clarify a meaning of a proposition, and want to do so by pursuing its definition further. A definition does not have a meaning, but it explains the meaning of a proposition (see PR 163). It is a rule, that is, a transformation rule. Namely, it states how a proposition is to be transformed into other propositions in which the unclarified concept no longer appears. It leads a concept back to others, and so forth, until the verification, which shows us the meaning, is attained (see W, 221). With that it explains the meaning, shows something that has a meaning.

'The definition *defines* something and it *shows* something. To a number there corresponds something which the definition shows.

'Can one define a form? Can one, for example, define the subject-predicate form as the class of all subject-predicate propositions? In such a definition the subject-predicate form itself would have to appear: in order to understand the definition we have to already know, therefore, what the subject-predicate form is. It is clear that we are dealing here not with actual propositions but with what makes it possible to form propositions.

'If a form were definable we could not understand it without definition. The possibility of expressing a meaning rests precisely upon our understanding a form without its being explained to us. The proposition shows its form. It is senseless to want to define *that* upon which the possibility of all communication and understanding rests.

'The error in this notion rests upon the fact that the form is understood as a *property*. One is of the opinion that the subject-predicate form is a universal property which all subject-predicate propositions have' (w, p. 224; see w, p. 220).

271   The proposition or sentence represents, and in representing it shows that it represents. This showing is not really hidden from us but we are again and again tempted to want to give a representation of it. 'If it is asked: "How do sentences manage to represent?" – the answer might be: "Don't you know? You certainly see it, when you use them."' For nothing is concealed.

'How do sentences do it? – Don't you know? For nothing is hidden' (PI 435).

N

WILL, RELIGION, ETHICS

I

272   The will is a sort of taking up of a position to the world (see NB, p. 86). Only within the framework of this taking up of a position do things in the world get their 'meaning' (see NB, p. 84). In this way things have their 'meaning' through their relation to my will. We understand 'meaning' here in the sense of 'meaning for our life'.

If the will is also a form of taking up a position to the world, it still refers to individual things in the world. The will has to have an object in the world. 'Otherwise we would have no foothold and could not know what we willed.

'And we could not will different things' (NB, p. 88). That is to say, if I do not will one thing, I can also not will another (see NB, p. 88).

273   My will fastens on to some place in the world. If I thereby move something I move myself. 'When I perform an action I am in action' (NB, p. 88).

II

274   Is the will an experience? In experience something is given to us. In what is given, however, we do not find the subject, and in willing we do find it. In experiencing, something happens, something is perceived, and in willing, something is not perceived, rather we do something. The will cannot be a phenomenon, for every phenomenon only *happens*, is perceived by us, but is not something that we *do*.

' "The will is not something which I see happen, but it consists as it were in our being in action; in our being the action." Look at your arm and move it and you experience that very strongly: "You do not observe how it moves, you do not have an experience – not merely an experience – but you *do* something." You can then say that you could very probably imagine the case that quite the same thing happens with your own hand, but observed by you, not willed by you. – But close your eyes and move your arm; then you also have an experience, and now ask yourself whether you could again imagine you were having the same experience but without willing it' (PG 97).

275   What leads us then to want to call the will or willing an experience? I cannot will willing. As if the willing of willing were a preparatory act of willing. It is as if with willing one had already willed and as if one still had not willed' (*Eine Philosophische Betrachtung, Schriften* 5, p. 236). I cannot always will, still if I do will, then I will. In a certain way I could therefore say: my willing simply happens. ' "Willing, too, is merely an experience", one would like to say (the "will" too only "idea"). It comes when it comes, and I cannot bring it about' (PI 611). But it does not happen to *me*, as an experience does, but it happens. And I am the one who wills. And if I observe myself in my willing, that is, if I want to have an experience, then I do not see my will but I see my acting (see BB, p. 151). However, I can bring about situations in which I have to will something. But that is not to will willing. 'In the sense in which I can never bring anything about (such as stomach ache through overeating), I can also bring about an act of willing. In this sense I bring about the act of willing to swim by jumping into the water. Doubtless I was trying to say: I can't will willing; that is, it makes no sense to speak of willing willing. "Willing" is not the name of an action' (PI 613).

276   Willing is immanent in acting itself. It does not evoke an action, it does not remain standing before acting; in a certain way it is acting itself (see PI 615). Willing is, to act intentionally. But the intention in which the action is done does not accompany the acting as little as the thought 'accompanies' the speaking (see PI, p. 529). It also does not precede the acting but is

found in acting itself. If, for example, I choose how to act, then no step precedes the choice, a step in which I would have the reason for my acting, but the choosing itself, and hence the action, is the reason. Another step cannot precede every step (see BB, p. 88).

III

277   There exists a gradual progression of willing which leads from the arbitrary will to the will that wills. In the case of the arbitrary will, what strikes our attention, as we could say, is the absence of the act of the will. In this way William James describes the act of getting up in the morning: 'He lies in bed and reflects whether it is already time to get up – and all at once *he finds that he is up*' (BB, p. 151).

Arbitrariness in the case of the absence of the will is not really directed against the will. I spontaneously do what I 'really' wanted. We also have cases of spontaneity 'in absence' of the will. For example, writing is movement and still spontaneously automatic. The hand is to some extent moved by a will that runs through it. 'The hand writes; it does not write because one wants to, but one wants what it writes' (z 586).

Another case of 'involuntary' is one in which there is no act of the will but in which we do something *against* our will. 'Crying out with pain against our will could be compared with raising our arm against our will when someone forces it up while we are struggling against him. But it is important to notice that the will – or should we say "wish" – not to cry out is over-come in a different way from that in which our resistance is overcome by the strength of the opponent. When we cry out against our will, we are as it were taken by surprise; as though someone forced up our hands by unexpectedly sticking a gun into our ribs, commanding "hands up" ' (BB, p. 155)!

Finally, the willing will can also be directed towards the future. Then I have an *intention*. An intention is a will that is directed towards a later will; an act of will which has as its object a later act of the will (see z 44–50).

278   The relational structure (*Zusammenhang*) 'voluntary-involuntary' shows us that the will is never totally absent from our life.

IV

279   I pursue in the world, through my will, various goals and purposes. A result of that is that my actions can be more or less 'good' (or 'bad' as less good), that is, 'good' in the relative sense exists in the world. But that means nothing else than that a certain, predefined goal or a certain predefined standard has been reached. Every value judgement which employs the relative concept of 'good' can, therefore, be transformed into a mere factual judgement. 'Every judgement of relative value is a mere statement of facts and can therefore be put in such a form that it loses all the appearance of a judgement of value: Instead of saying: "This is the right way to Grantchester", I could equally well have said: "This is the right way you have to go if you want to get to Grantchester in the shortest time"' (E, p. 6).

280   In the world there are only facts. And no determination of facts can be or imply an absolute value judgement. In the world there is no value. A value has to be something on which I have to be able to rely. Therefore, it cannot be contingent. In the world, however, everything is contingent. Therefore, value has to be found outside the world. 'The sense of the world must lie outside the world. In the world everything is as it is, and everything happens as it does happen; *in* it no value exists – and if it did exist it would have no value.

'If there is any value that does have value, it must lie outside the whole sphere of what happens and is the case. For all that happens and is the case is accidental.

'What makes it non-accidental cannot lie *within* the world, since if it did it would itself be accidental.

'It must lie outside the world' (T 6.41).

281   If there did exist an absolute value in the world, then I could not at all will it in some way. For my will has to have, as

we saw, an object in the world which I can will or not. To willing there belongs the possibility of not-willing. An absolutely correct way would be a way which everyone would necessarily have to go. 'We would have to will' the absolute good. It would be something that everyone without reference to taste, inclinations, and so on, would have to accomplish. 'And I want to say that such a state of affairs is a chimera. No state of affairs has, in itself, what I would like to call the coercive power of an absolute judge' (E, p. 7).

V

282   My will is my attitude *to* the world. It is the bearer of good and evil (see NB, p. 76). I cannot make the world. 'The world is *given* to me, that is, my will enters into the world completely from outside as into something that is already there' (NB, p. 74). I cannot therefore make the world but only work on it and hence I alter it in single cases. But the good and evil willing have no effect on the facts in the world, for in the world there is no value. The willing of good or of evil only has an effect on the *limit*s of the world (see T 6.43). Just as my language means the world, and its limits are the limits of my world, so my attitude means the world and it alters from time to time its boundaries, for it concerns the world at any given time *as a whole*. I do not do certain things with my will but I do all things with a certain will. 'In short, the world must then become a wholly different one. The world must, so to speak, wax or wane as a whole. As if by the accession or loss of meaning' (NB, p. 73). It is not the world which is good or evil, but only the I (see NB, p. 79). Because the subject is not part of the world but is the limit of the world, good and evil willing have no effect on the world or in the world, but on the limits of the world, on the world as a whole.

283   'Good' and 'evil', 'happy' and 'unhappy' are related concepts. Because in the world there does not exist any values but only facts, the world is a different world if I am happy or unhappy. In a certain way one could even say: good and evil do not exist, there is only happy or unhappy (see NB, p. 74).

The happy life appears in a certain way more balanced, more harmonious than the unhappy (see NB, p. 78).

If my conscience disturbs my equilibrium then that means that I am not in agreement with something.

Still, when I am happy I cannot describe to what extent the world has altered. 'The solution of the problem of life is seen in the vanishing of the problem.

'(Is not this the reason why those who have found after a long period of doubt that the sense of life became clear to them have then been unable to say what constituted that sense?)' (T 6.521.)

284   Can one live in such a way that life ceases to be problematical? Can one live in the eternal and not in time? Can one be happy in spite of the misery of the world which one just cannot ward off?

The life of knowing is a constant striving for agreement, a constant effecting of agreement. Therefore the life of knowing is the life which is happy (see NB, pp. 73, 81f).

285   World and life are one (see T 5.621).

We do not mean life here in either a physiological or a psychological sense (see NB, p. 77). My will can only will the world just as my language can only mean the world. Both permeate one another. Therefore, world and life are one, therefore, life is the world.

286   Being happy, agreement between will and world, cannot mean that we accept the facts of the world. Life cannot be something contingent. But if its contingency is supposed to be abolished, then that cannot happen through the world or through something which is in the world (see PR 47). For in the world everything is contingent.

VI

287   Since in the world there are only facts, one cannot speak about value in meaningful propositions. Still, there are three experiences in which the absolute appears and which we try to

express. Whenever we speak of 'absolute good' or of an 'absolute value' we have such experiences in mind.

The first experience, perhaps the experience par excellence, is being astonished that the world exists.

When we normally speak of 'being astonished', then we have something rare or extraordinary in view. But in all cases it is something we can imagine were not the case. Now we saw earlier that in order to be able to give a sense to a positive proposition we have to be able to give a sense to the corresponding negative proposition (see T 5.515).

'But it is nonsense to say that I wonder at the existence of the world, because I cannot imagine it not existing. I would of course wonder at the world round me being as it is. If for instance I had this experience while looking into the blue sky, I could wonder at the sky being blue as opposed to the case when it's clouded. But that's not what I mean. I am wondering at the sky being *whatever it is*' (E, p. 9).

One could perhaps want to say that in this case we are astonished at a tautology. But it would be nonsense to say this because it is impossible to be astonished at a tautology, because everything lies open.

288   The second experience is that 'of feeling *absolutely* safe. I mean the state of mind in which one is inclined to say: "I am safe, nothing can injure me whatever happens"' (E, p. 8). I say that I am secure if the circumstances hinder certain things from happening to me. It is of course nonsense to say: I am secure *no matter what may happen*.

289   The third experience is that of being guilty. Certainly I can have the feeling of guilt if I have not done something which I should have done. But what corresponds to the feeling that I totally and universally do not do what I have to do, that I do not satisfy my obligation, *no matter what I do*, that I am purely and simply guilty?

VII

290   Within the framework of a large and complicated allegory religious language transforms these experiences about which we

can only speak in non-sensical propositions into statements
about meaningful facts. 'But this allegory also describes the
experience which I have just referred to. For the first of them is,
I believe, exactly what people were referring to when they said
that God had created the world; and the experience of absolute
safety has been described by saying that we feel safe in the
hands of God. A third experience of the same kind is that of
feeling guilty and again this was described by the phrase that
God disapproves of our conduct' (E, p. 10).

291   In religious language we can also understand the 'good'.
In that language the good is not just 'the good' which again
would have to be grounded, but it is what God orders. 'Simply
put, there were in theological ethics two conceptions of the
essence of good: according to the superficial interpretation the
good is good for the reason that God wills it; according to the
deeper interpretation God wills the good because it is good.
I am of the opinion that the first conception is the deeper: the
good is what God orders. For it cuts off the path of every
explanation "why" it is good, while precisely the second conception is the superficial, rationalistic one, which acts "as if"
what is good still could be grounded.
   'The first conception clearly says that the essence of the good
has nothing to do with facts and accordingly cannot be explained by any proposition. If there exists a proposition which
expresses just what I mean, it is the proposition: the good is
what God orders' (w, p. 115).

292   The three experiences in which the Absolute, therefore
absolute value, therefore the good, appears to us, have to do
with God. Therefore the sense of the world, which has to lie
outside of it, has to do with God.
   'God and the purpose of life?
   'I know that this world exists.
   'That I am placed in it like my eye in its visual field.
   'That something about it is problematical which we call its
meaning.
   'That this meaning does not lie in it but outside it.
   'That life is the world.
   'That my will penetrates the world.

'That my will is good or evil.

'Therefore that good and evil are somehow connected with the meaning of the world.

'The meaning of life, i.e., the meaning of the world, we can call God.

'And connect with this the comparison of God to a father.

'To pray is to think about the meaning of life . . .

'To believe in a god means to see that the facts of the world are not the end of the matter.

'To believe in God means to see that life has a meaning' (NB, pp. 72, 73, 74).

VIII

293   We seem to constantly use analogies in the language of ethics and religion. But analogies are analogies *for* something. They would have to be able, therefore, to be interpreted and translated. Here, however, the analogies do not stand for something else but for themselves. Just as I am amazed in being astonished not about anything whatsoever but about the existence of the world itself, just as I see the existence of the world as a marvel, just as the world stands there independently and still astonishes us, so that while being in the world we are beyond it, in the same way, when using analogies, we are beyond them. Precisely by not pointing beyond themselves, the analogies point beyond themselves in an inexpressible fashion.

We cannot meaningfully express what is found in the analogies and points beyond them, any more than we can meaningfully express the wonder of the existence of the world. Sometimes we would like to express this wonder through the wonder of language itself. The expression for the wonder of the world would be the existence of language itself. But the existence of language itself is a wonder that I cannot express. I can say something in language, but the existence of language does not express anything, it says nothing. Language cannot say itself in its existence, for it would then have to be outside of itself. 'For all I have said by shifting the expression of the miraculous from an expression *by means of* language and to the expression *by the existence* of language, all I have said is again that we cannot express what we want to express and that all we *say* about the absolute miraculous remains nonsense' (E, p. 11).

294   When we are discoursing in religion and in ethics we are dealing with a flash of insight (*Aufblitzen*) which really cannot be described: so every description in those domains is absurd for the very reason that it wants to express the inexpressible. 'That is to say: I see now that these nonsensical expressions were not nonsensical because I had yet found the correct expressions, but that their nonsensicality was their very essence. For all I wanted to do with them was just *to go beyond* the world and that is to say beyond significant language' (E, p. 11).

295   Because the world exists, there is something which exists beyond the world and which is unutterable: the mystical. 'It is not *how* things are in the world that is mystical, but *that* it exists' (T 6.44). 'There are, indeed, things that cannot be put into words. They *make themselves manifest*. They are what is mystical' (T 6.522).

IX

296   Ethics, in so far as it wants to say something about the final meaning of life and about the 'absolute good', the 'absolutely worthwhile', cannot be a science (see E, p. 12).

297   Just as logic does not deal with the world but is the condition for our being able to speak about the world, so also ethics does not treat of the world but is the condition for our being able to act meaningfully in the world (see NB, p. 77). It asks about what is 'good' and what is 'valuable'; about what really matters; about the sense of life; about the right way to live (see E, p. 12).

298   By 'meaning' (*Sinn*) we understand here not what we have described as the meaning of a proposition, but the 'meaning' (*Bedeutung*) for our life.

O

REMARKS ON PHILOSOPHY

I

299 'Man has the impulse to run up against the limits of language' (w, p. 68). And philosophy stems from that. Going beyond language, man wants constantly to say what cannot be said. This running-up-against becomes manifest in amazement. There is nothing more self-evident than that I exist and that the world exists. And still I am amazed about the world's existing. I speak and still I am amazed that I do speak. Amazement is not a question; it also cannot be expressed as a question; and there is no answer to it. It is the self-manifestation of the limit.

300 'The results of philosophy are the uncovering of one or another piece of plain nonsense and of bumps that the understanding has got by running its head up against the limits of language. These bumps make us see the value of the discovery' (PI 119).

'What is your aim in philosophy? – To show the fly the way out of the fly bottle' (PI 309).

So the goal of philosophy is, therefore, to heal bumps, to eliminate misunderstandings, to show ways out. Genuine understanding is already given to us in some way beforehand. But it is skewed and distorted. We do not need, therefore, first to create a genuine understanding, or rather we create it by the very fact that we eliminate misunderstandings, untie knots. Moreover, we can do that only because genuine understanding is already in some way present (see PG 72).

301 Philosophy is concerned with tracing the limits of language and therefore of thought *from within.*

N

'It must set limits to what can be thought; and, by doing so, to what cannot be thought. It must set limits to what cannot be thought by working outwards through what can be thought. It will signify what cannot be said, by presenting what can be said' (T 4.114, 4.115).

II

302   The misunderstandings with which we have to do are not practical misunderstandings which we could avoid by improving our terminology. In such a case language is joined completely with reality, it is in agreement with it. The misunderstandings which we want to eliminate arise from language's not striking into reality. 'The confusions which occupy us arise when language is like an engine idling, not when it is doing work' (PI 132).

303   Such an idling exists, for example, when we see a law in the way in which a word is used. In striving to apply the law coherently, paradoxical results arise. Let us take, for example, the question: 'What is time?' It gives the impression that a definition is being asked for. If we then give one, that does not help us out of the embarrassment but first brings us really into it. The coherent application of a definition that has been given first off, e.g., 'time is the movement of heavenly bodies', leads us in fact to paradoxical results. We let ourselves be taken captive by certain forms of expression and have to fight ourselves free of them. We do that by not leaving the forms of expression undecided, but by investigating the concepts which are found in them, in order to see how they are or can be applied.

'Philosophy, as we use the word, is a fight against the fascination which forms of expression exert upon us' (BB, p. 27).

In this sense philosophical investigations are conceptual investigations (see Z 458).

304   Many problems arise through false simplications, as when we believe that beauty is contained in a beautiful thing as alcohol is contained in a bottle (see BB, p. 144).

III

305   Another confusion arises through my referring emphatically to something specific. If by means of a false language use I divide off this specific element as a separate thing from that which it characterizes, I cannot say any longer what the issue is. Let us assume, for example, that someone has a special way of sitting, and I want to sketch him 'this way'. Just as the expression 'this proposition' points to a proposition which itself has to be expressed, so 'this way' is not something independent but points to something which happens in this way.

'I've now been observing the way A sits and smokes. I want to draw him like this. In this case I needn't be ready to give any description of a particular feature of his attitude, and my statement may just mean: "I've been observing A as he sat and smoked." – "The way" can't in this case be separated from him. Now if I wished to draw him as he sat there, and was contemplating, studying his attitude, I should while doing so be inclined to say and repeat to myself: "He has a particular way of sitting." But the answer to the question "What way?" would be "Well, *this* way", and perhaps one would give it by drawing the characteristic outlines of his attitude. On the other hand, my phrase "He has a particular way. . . .", might just have to be translated into "I'm contemplating his attitude." Putting it in this form we have, as it were, straightened out the proposition; whereas in its first form its meaning seems to describe a loop, that is to say, the word "particular" here seems to be used transitively and, more particularly, reflexively, i.e., we are regarding its use as a special case of the transitive use. We are inclined to answer the question "What way do you mean?" by "*This* way", instead of answering: "I didn't refer to any particular feature; I was just contemplating his position." My expression made it appear as though I was pointing out something *about* his way of sitting, or, in our previous case, about the way the word "red" came, whereas what makes me use the word "particular" here is that by my attitude towards the phenomenon I am laying an emphasis on it: I am concentrating on it, or retracing it in my mind, or drawing it, etc.

'Now this is a characteristic situation to find ourselves in when thinking about philosophical problems. There are many troubles which arise in this way, that a word has a transitive and an intransitive use, and that we regard the latter as a particular case of the former, explaining the word when it is used intransitively by a reflexive construction' (BB, p. 160).

I exchange the expression 'by A I mean B' in which B is an explanation for A, for an expression in which I only apparently say: 'by A I mean B'; but in which B really is a repetition of A and with which it is said that there is no further explanation for A.

'Thus we say: "By 'kilogram' I mean the weight of one litre of water", "By 'A' I mean 'B', where B is an explanation of A." But there is also the intransitive use: "I said that I was sick of it and meant it." Here again, meaning what you said could be called "retracing it", "laying an emphasis on it". But using the word "meaning" in this sentence makes it appear that it must have sense to ask: "*What* did you mean?" and to answer: "By what I said I meant what I said", treating the case of "I mean what I say" as a special case of "By saying 'A' I mean 'B'." In fact one uses the expression "I mean what I mean" to say: "I have no explanation for it." The question "What does this sentence p mean?" if it doesn't ask for a translation of p into other symbols, has no more sense than "What sentence is formed by this sequence of words?"

'Suppose to the question: "What's a kilogram?" I answered: "It is what a litre of water weighs", and someone asked: "Well, what does a litre of water weigh?" –

'We often use the reflexive form of speech as a means of emphasizing something. And in all such cases the reflexive expressions can be "straightened out". Thus we use the expression "If I can't, I can't", "I am as I am", "It is just what it is", also "that's that" ' (BB, pp. 160–1).

306   Finally, analogies can lead us into error, that is, by our overlooking that an expression has several meanings, and we then falsely apply one meaning where we should have used another.

'It is, in most cases, impossible to show an exact point where an analogy begins to mislead us. Every particular notation stresses some particular point of view. If, e.g., we call our investigations "philosophy", this title, on the one hand, seems appropriate, on the other hand it certainly has misled people (One might say that the subject we are dealing with is one of the heirs of the subject which used to be called "philosophy".). The cases in which particularly we wish to say that someone is misled by a form of expression are those in which we would say: "he wouldn't talk as he does if he were aware of this difference in the grammar of such-and-such words, or if he were aware of this other possibility of expression" and so on. Thus we may say of some philosophizing mathematicians that they are obviously not aware of the difference between the many different usages of the word "proof"; and that they are not clear about the difference between the uses of the word "kind", when they talk of kinds of numbers, kinds of proofs, as though the word "kind" here meant the same thing as in the context "kinds of apples". Or, we may say, they are not aware of the different *meanings* of the word "discovery", when in one case we talk of the discovery of the construction of the pentagon and in the other case of the discovery of the South Pole' (BB, pp. 28–9).

IV

307 Philosophy must show that there is no problem where there really is none (see PG 9).

Confusing problems, for example, can arise through my excluding elements from a language-game without which this game is no longer intelligible. For example, if I treated the past, present and future as not belonging to the same time, a confusing problem arises if I want to measure an interval of time.

'If we treat a definite philosophical problem, something like: "How is it possible to measure an interval of time since past and future are not present and the present is only a point?" – what is characteristic about that is that here a confusion is expressed in the form of a question which does not recognize this confusion. That the questioner will be *released* by a definite change of his manner of expression' (PG 141).

Or I introduce elements into a game, where they have no business at all, as, for example, 'silent notes' into the playing of the organ. Then again confusion arises and not a genuine problem.

I could imagine an organ whose stops were to be operated by keys which were completely identical in form to the keys of the keyboard and were dispersed among them. And there could now arise a philosophical problem: 'how are silent notes possible?' And the one to solve the problem would be the one who saw that the stop keys were to be replaced by pull-stops which had no resemblance to the keyboard.

'A philosophically analogous problem, or uneasiness, could arise, say, through the fact that someone *played* on all the keys of the keyboard, that the result did not sound like music, and that he was still tempted to think it *had* to be music, etc.' (PG 141).

V

308 Another kind of misunderstanding lies in the fact that very often the unhidden ground of something lies before us, that we see it, that, however, we would nevertheless like to develop it still further. It seems to us that we would have to first still hold onto something, stabilize it (*'fest' stellen*) as it were, and that it is a matter of appearances that are difficult to grasp, which rapidly slip away, and that we would have to get a hold of the flow of appearances in order to see it more precisely. That points toward the fact that here a false application of language is suggesting something false (see PR 52; PG 120).

VI

309 A source of obscurities lies in our prejudice in favour of the method of the natural sciences, that is, in our wanting to join problems together by means of generalizing hypotheses. 'Philosophers constantly see the method of science before their eyes, and are irresistibly tempted to ask and answer questions in the way science does. This tendency is the real source of metaphysics, and leads the philosopher into complete darkness. I want to say here that it can never be our job to reduce anything. Philosophy really *is* "purely descriptive"' (BB, p. 18).

VII

310   In philosophy no hypotheses are formed, no inferences drawn, no assertions made. One does not say: 'this is the way it has to be', but how things are shown. The overcoming of misunderstandings happens by means of description.

'In philosophy we do not draw conclusions. "But it must be like this!" is not a philosophical proposition. Philosophy only states what everyone admits (. . .). Philosophy may in no way interfere with the actual use of language; it can in the end only describe it.

'For it cannot give it any foundation either.

'It leaves everything as it is (. . .).

'Philosophy simply puts everything before us, and neither explains nor deduces anything. – Since everything lies open to view there is nothing to explain. For what is hidden, for example, is of no interest to us.

'One might also give the name "philosophy" to what is possible *before* all new discoveries and inventions' (PI 599, 124, 126).

It is difficult to find the proper beginning or rather not to want to go once again behind this beginning when one has found it (see OC 471). The difficulty is to accept something as a solution which first looks like a preliminary step towards it. The difficulty is: to stop (see Z 312, 314, see above, No. 257).

VIII

311   If philosophy, nevertheless, is not simple but complex, then it is that only because of the knots which we have put into thinking and which we have to untie now in a complicated fashion. 'Why is philosophy so complicated? It should indeed be *completely* simple. – Philosophy looses the knots in our thinking which we have unknowingly put there: in that regard it has to make movements just as complicated as these knots. Although, therefore, the *result* of philosophy is simple, its method of arriving at it cannot be.

'The complexity of philosophy is not that of its material but that of our knotted understanding' (PR 2).

312   Add to this the dark background of our thoughts, which has to be illuminated and expressed time and again. 'Behind our thoughts, true and false, there is found again and again a dark ground which we can only later draw into the light and express as a thought' (NB, p. 125).

We try in this way again and again to express what is not yet to be expressed, but cannot say what we really want to say (see OC 400). That a first expression, however, may be false still does not mean that we are in the wrong. We have to then try further to create clarity, 'just as one who rightly criticizes a picture often will first bring the criticism to bear where it does not belong, and there is need of an *investigation* to find the right point to place the blame' (OC 37).

'A philosophical problem has the form: "I don't know my way about" ' (PI 123).

'One of the most difficult tasks of the philosopher is to find where the shoe pinches him' (NB, p. 60).

Sometimes a philosophical thought is so soft that it is already drowned out and no longer heard when one is asked about it and is supposed to speak about it (see Z 453).

313   Therefore, a philosopher has to treat a question like an illness. He must not cut off the thought illness but must lead it slowly along the natural path of healing. In doing so he has to take care that he does not overlook a cause of the illness: the one-sided diet, being nourished with only one kind of example (see PI 255; Z 382; PI 593).

IX

314   Because philosophy wants to create clarity by means of description it treats problems and not *a* problem. A 'universal' principle is, therefore, not essential to it. It has to do with the concept of a calculus as well as with the concept of a thought, of propositions, of language. But if it essentially had to do with the concept of a calculus, therefore with the calculus of all calculi – instead of the representation of calculi – then behind philosophy there would be still another philosophy, a metaphilosophy. But there is no such thing (see PG 72).

There is no one *principle*, no one *method*, which would arise from concepts of concepts, but there are various methods, as it were, various therapies, because philosophy does not hold itself to one principle, but to the fundamental proposition of describing reality (see PI 133).

Because I do not have to be constantly occupied with what the one problem of philosophy is, and whether it really is *the* problem of philosophy and whether it is not itself put into question, I can do philosophy in peace. 'The discovery is the one that makes me capable of stopping doing philosophy when I want to. – The one that gives philosophy peace, so that it is no longer tormented by questions which bring *itself* into question. – Instead, we now demonstrate a method, by examples, and the series of examples can be broken off. – Problems are solved (difficulties eliminated), not a *single* problem' (PI 133).

X

315   Accordingly, the most important thing we are striving after is clarity, order, and perspicuity, for they are clearly missing. The general view of the whole is the great problem. Not exactness and full brightness are to be first striven for, but perspicuity (see NB, p. 23; z 464).

'A main source of our failure to understand is that we do not *command a clear view* of the use of our words. – Our grammar is lacking in this sort of perspicuity. A perspicuous representation produces just that understanding which consists in 'seeing connections''. Hence the importance of finding and inventing *intermediate cases*.

'The concept of a perspicuous representation is of fundamental significance for us. It earmarks the form of account we give, the way we look at things. (Is this a '*Weltanschauung*''?)' (PI 122).

XI

316   Because in philosophy we handle many cases with many different methods, we have to go piece by piece, stretch by stretch, and cannot grasp everything at once.

'Uneasiness in philosophy, one could say, comes because we look upon philosophy in the wrong way, see it in the wrong way, as it were, that is, tear it into (endless) longitudinal strips instead of into (limited) cross-sections. This false approach creates the *greatest* difficulty. We want, therefore, as it were, to grasp the unlimited longitudinal strip and complain that it is not piece by piece possible. Certainly not if by a piece one understands a strip which is literally infinite. But it is possible, if by that one understands a limited cross-section. – But then we again do not come to an end of our labour! – Certainly not, for it has none' (z 447).

317   If we have grasped a cross-section, then we have solved a philosophical problem. With the solution also of only one philosophical problem we have reached something definitive. It is, namely, a partial result. Perhaps it has not yet found a definitive place in a greater system. This place can be changed, under circumstances, after the solution of other problems, that is, by other partial results. What is important, however, is that the solution have its own validity, proportionate to how many problems still remain to be solved and proportionate to what place it then will assume among the further solved problems. One says sometimes 'that no philosophical problem can be solved until all philosophical problems are solved; which means that as long as they aren't all solved every new difficulty renders all our previous results questionable. To this statement we can only give a rough answer if we are to speak about philosophy in such general terms. It is, that every new problem which arises may put in question the *position* which our previous partial results are to occupy in the final picture. One then speaks of having to reinterpret these previous results; and we should say: they have to be placed in a different surrounding.

'Imagine we had to arrange the books of a library. When we

begin the books lie higgeldy-piggeldy on the floor. Now there would be many ways of sorting them and putting them in their places. One would be able to take the books one by one and put each on the shelf in its right place. On the other hand we might take up several books from the floor and put them in a row on a shelf, merely in order to indicate that these books ought to go together in this order. In the course of arranging the library this whole row of books will have to change its place. But it would be wrong to say that therefore putting them together on a shelf was no step towards the final result. In this case, it fact, it is pretty obvious that having put together books which belong was a definite achievement, even though the whole row of them had to be shifted. But some of the greatest achievements in philosophy could only be compared with taking up some books which seemed to belong together, and putting them on different shelves; nothing more being final about their positions than that they no longer lie side by side. The onlooker who doesn't know the difficulty of the task might well think in such a case nothing at all had been achieved. – The difficulty in philosophy is to say no more than we know. E.g., to see that when we have put two books together in their right order we have not thereby put them in their final places' (BB, pp. 44–5).

If we have learned in this way to take a step, then we notice we have the possibility of going a distance (see PR 165).

The many cross-sections which we have to grasp are like the pieces of a jigsaw puzzle: they are all present, only all mixed up. 'And there is a further analogy between the jigsaw puzzle and our case: It's no use trying to apply force in fitting pieces together. All we should do is to look at them *carefully* and arrange them' (BB, p. 46).

XII

318 Philosophy is therefore no theory, something with dogmas, and so on, but it is an activity. It *deals with* reality as it is simultaneously given to us and distorted in language. Therefore, a philosophical work essentially consists of explications (see T 4.112).

Philosophy consists just in this activity. If philosophy thereby

178   *Remarks on Philosophy*

represents itself, applies the word 'philosophy' to itself, there is still no metaphilosophy on this account. 'One might think: if philosophy speaks of the use of a word "philosophy" there must be a second-order philosophy. But it is not so: it is, rather, like the case of orthography, which deals with the word "orthography" among others without then being second-order' (PI 121).

INDEX OF CITATIONS AND REFERENCES

The abbreviations, which refer to works of Wittgenstein, are listed on p. xvii of this volume. Each original work mentioned in the Foreword is given with the relevant paragraph or page number of the original. In the index to subject chapters of this book, the first number in each entry refers to a paragraph in this book; the numbers that follow cite numbered paragraphs, or, where specified, pages of the works in which Wittgenstein discussed the topic.